T0105677

# ANSWERS
# TO
# QUESTIONS

## You always wanted to know about Christianity*

**\*BUT WERE AFRAID TO ASK**

*Betty W. O'Berry*

WestBow
PRESS
A DIVISION OF THOMAS NELSON

WestBow Press books may be ordered through booksellers or by contacting:

WestBow Press
A Division of Thomas Nelson
1663 Liberty Drive
Bloomington, IN 47403
www.westbowpress.com
1-(866) 928-1240

Because of the dynamic nature of the Internet, any web addresses or links contained in this book may have changed since publication and may no longer be valid. The views expressed in this work are solely those of the author and do not necessarily reflect the views of the publisher, and the publisher hereby disclaims any responsibility for them.

Any people depicted in stock imagery provided by Thinkstock are models, and such images are being used for illustrative purposes only.

Certain stock imagery © Thinkstock.

ISBN: 978-1-4497-5521-8 (sc)
ISBN: 978-1-4497-5522-5 (e)

Library of Congress Control Number: 2012915757

Printed in the United States of America

WestBow Press rev. date: 10/30/2012

In loving memory of my late husband,

Fred Bernard O'Berry, Jr.

Who loved me and was resolute in
helping me be all I could be.

# TABLE OF CONTENTS

# Foreword

Betty O'Berry has been a close friend and sister in the Lord for over thirty years. I have a very high regard for her. It is a pleasure to write the foreword to her new book. Betty is a widow, a mother, an artist, a poet, and a writer. Her greatest love is for God and for His people.

I highly recommend this book because I know Betty has put her heart into every word. I could say "This is your life, Betty O' Berry." This book contains her life encounters with God and people. The information she desires to share, the questions people would like to ask, but never do, and the answers that are needed to live for the Lord Jesus Christ are contained within the pages of this book. I can tell you that she is a woman of God and a woman of integrity.

Betty has lived the life that God's word tells us we must live. Jesus told the apostle Paul that he would suffer many tests, trials, and persecutions in his life. Most of our trials and persecutions will come from friends, family, people we meet in every day life, and the religious world. These are the things that seem to hurt the most. She has lived life like all of us, trying to do it all right, and seemed to be failing at every turn, but God never failed. It seems that not only Betty, but all of us go through the same things in life. This book contains questions for which she sought answers, answers she accumulated from years of studying God's Word, and the wisdom she gained by living a life devoted to God.

Betty has made all the same mistakes that we all make. I can say with all my heart that Betty O'Berry has done her best with God as the center point in all that she has done, with the information she had from the start, and what she has gleaned from God of living life for Him. With a life of work, much prayer, patience, and tears, she is fighting the fight, she is still running the race, and now she is waiting to hear her master say, "Well done, good and faithful servant."

This Book will be an inspiration to you and much help in your life. I highly recommend it. It's good stuff.

A Friend and brother in Christ,

Rev. Richard Black

# PREFACE

Everyday we are bombarded with thoughts that cause us to doubt our Christian Faith. How many of you have heard statements such as these: "How do you know there is a God?" "All religions serve the same God we serve." "It doesn't matter what you believe, as long as you believe something." "The Bible is just another book that is so old and outdated it doesn't apply to our lives today." "Jesus was a good man and a great teacher, but anyone who believes He is the only way to God is narrow-minded and mean-spirited." "There is no such thing as sin; people have mental problems and disease." So the silent majority listens and stays silent because they don't know why they are right. God forbid if someone should think they are politically incorrect or narrow-minded.

It seems many Christians have never been taught the basics. If you ask the average Christian what they believe and why, and give them ten minutes to answer, you probably would get answers such as these: "I have gone to church all my life." "I have always been a Christian." "I believe in God." "I believe the Bible." "I believe in Jesus and have been baptized." They have no knowledge of why they believe as they do. It is just what people are supposed to say if they are a Christian. Then someone comes along with what appears to be a genuine love for them and gives them information that seemingly contradicts what they do not know, so they can easily be led down a path where they no longer believe that Jesus was really God manifested in the flesh. Someone can tell them the Bible has been translated so many times and is full of errors, and they believe them. They usually claim they have a better Bible which contains a better, or later, revelation; and the unwary believe them. Because of not knowing the truth of the Word of God, or why they believe, many are deceived into serving a god who is not the God of the Bible.

The purpose of this book is to answer questions for someone who is not a believer, for a believer who needs to have these questions answered for them, and to lay a foundation of truth for the man or woman of God. It is my belief that if we can truly believe these truths and understand them, not only would we be willing to die for our faith, we will also have a solid foundation on which to live a victorious Christian life. We would not easily be swayed to and fro by every wind of doctrine. The winds and storms of life may assail us, but we will have built our house of faith on the solid rock of the Word of God, which will stand any onslaught the devil might bring.

This information is very elementary and simple, yet it is the very foundation of our Christian beliefs. It is primarily designed to introduce Christians to the terminology and basic teachings of what we believe and why. When the foundation is built, it is easy to add to the structure. There is no way everything that needs to be said about a particular subject can be addressed in this book. We will be moving through some very important subjects at a rather fast pace. Take time to reflect on what you read.

Anyone who is serious about wanting to know the basics of Christianity, interested in laying a firm foundation, and wanting to mature in the Lord should gain much insight from this material.

## Hebrews 5:12-6:3

*For though by this time you ought to be teachers, you need someone to teach you again the first principles of the oracles of God; and you have come to need milk and not solid food. For everyone who partakes only of milk is unskilled in the word of righteousness, for he is a babe. But solid food belongs to those who are of full age, that is, those who by reason of use have their senses exercised to discern both good and evil. Therefore, leaving the discussion of the elementary principles of Christ, let us go on to perfection, not laying again the foundation of repentance from dead works and of faith toward God, the doctrine of baptisms, of laying on of hands, of resurrection of the dead, and of eternal judgment. And this we will do if God permits.*

# Acknowledgements:

To Drs. Lynn & Linda Reddick, pastors at Church on the Way, for their help in editing my manuscript for grammatical and scriptural errors. My heartfelt gratitude also goes to Gloria Jenkins, Gail Sanders, Martha Trapnell, and especially Carie Olsen whose help in the final editing and whose encouragement was invaluable to me.

To my dear friend, Rev. Richard E. Black, who was more confident of God in me than I thought was in myself. He helped verify my material for content and spiritual insight.

To all my family and friends who encouraged me and believed that God has given me something valuable to share with a lost and dying world.

To the myriad of preachers and teachers who have touched my life and from whom I gleaned so much of the information I now pass on to you.

# Chapter One

## HOW DO YOU KNOW THERE IS A GOD?

A merica has slowly but systematically removed the concept of the God of the Bible from our society. There is no mention of God in our schools, and God is only ridiculed on many of the popular television programs. Sin has now become a "disease," and we are being taught that the world was created through evolution. The average person fills their mind every waking hour with music or television; or else they are involved with some type of entertainment and are never still and silent long enough to contemplate who they are, where they came from, and what their purpose is here on earth. Since our very lives, the lives of our loved ones, and the future of the world hang in the balance, what we believe about God is vital. Which brings us to the question, "How do we know there is a God?" "What does the Holy Bible have to say about God?" "The fool has said in his heart there is no God."[1] "Since the creation of the world, His invisible attributes are clearly seen, being understood by the things that are made, even His eternal power and godhead so they are without excuse." [2] "Without faith it is impossible to please Him: for he that cometh to God must believe that He is and that He rewards them that diligently seek him."[3] From these verses we see that everyone knows, innately, that there is a God, and only a fool would say in his heart there is no God. I can speak with authority and tell you, anyone who believes there is a God and seeks Him, will find Him if he seeks Him with his whole heart.

### For further evidence here are more proofs that God exists:

This is a quote from the foreword of a typical college textbook, which discards the Biblical record of creation: "Our own galaxy, which we remember is but a tiny part of the universe, has probably existed a million years. But some progress has been made in attempting to explain how and when the sun and its nine planets came into being. The study of the solar system gives us at least a clue to the origin of that part of the universe most important to us, the earth. The explanation commonly accepted today is called the Hypothesis (we guess) of Dynamic Encounter. I.C. Chamberlain and F.R. Moulton of the University of Chicago formulated it about 1900. In brief it suggests that our solar system had its birth when the sun was approached by another huge star. The latter, through the operation of the law of gravitation, detached from the sun great masses of flaming gas. The orphan masses from the parent sun gradually cooled and crystallized to become the nuclei of planets. These continued to revolve around the sun, held in their orbits by the gravitational pull of the parent body. The evolution of the earth to its present state was very gradual."[4]

What a fantastic array! An entire universe—a whole solar system, a huge sun, and the operation of certain, definite, immutable, unchangeable laws is supposed to exist from a supposed collision between gigantic, breathtaking, huge, astral bodies! Think of all the laws that exist for this to have happened: heat, light, energy, motion, the rotation of astral bodies, the law of gravity, and others too numerous to mention. Scientists and astronomers tell us that our solar system is only one of many such systems in our great galaxy called the Milky Way, and that we are merely a third rate planet in a second rate solar system lost in the expanses of seemingly limitless space! Do you begin to comprehend that someone had to have already established these laws? By what law did one star approach another? By what law did heat gradually cool? By what law was there a gravitational pull? With a closer look at this hypothesis, we begin to see that in every case the writers have begun with an orderly, law-abiding universe, governed by irrefutable laws. The existence of Laws, unchangeable, immutable, irrevocable, unseen, and yet active, absolutely demands the existence of a great lawgiver! There is one lawgiver who is able to save and to destroy.[5] **Our God is the great lawgiver!**

The Theory (we think) of Evolution states simply that all forms that we know today, including humankind, all plant and animal life in its entire myriad species, have gradually evolved from the most simple life forms to the complex intricate interdependent species we see about us today; each having its own peculiar cyclical life character, each reproducing according to its kind. There is not the slightest evidence that life can come from the non-living, however, there is an absolute demonstrable law of science, which comprises the second major proof of the existence of a life-giving God, the Law of biogenesis. "Bio" means life. "Genesis" means beginning.

The law simply states "life comes only from life." The non living can never give rise to, give birth to, or produce the living! The very existence of life demands a life giver. Genesis 2:7 states, "And the eternal God formed man of the dust of the ground and breathed into his nostrils the breath of life, and man became a living soul." Acts 17:28 tells us that "In Him we live and move and have our being." Almighty God (the Life, Self-existent, the One who has life, who is life, who was before all things) imparted life to the first man and set within man, the animals and all plants, the cyclical character of life which enables them to reproduce according to a certain set of laws! **Our God is the great life giver!**

Matter occupies space and has weight. Certain gases and even the air we breathe are also classified as matter. Science has proved that this earth is gradually running down! Observe the erosion of fields, mountains, valleys, and various topographical features about you. Matter must have at one time come into existence, since by its very nature it has existed in past eternity. Colossians 1:15-17 tells us, "He is the image of the invisible God, the firstborn over all creation. For by Him all things were created that are in heaven and that are on earth, visible and invisible, whether thrones or dominions or principalities or powers. All things were created through Him and for Him. And He is before all things, and in Him all things consist." Creation then, the very existence of things, absolutely demands and requires a creator. That which is made requires a maker. That which is produced requires a producer. "In the beginning God created the heavens and the earth."[6] **Our God is the great creator!**

Evolutionists theorize (think) that man was once a one-cell amoeba that came out of the sea. In attempting to prove their case, they have arrayed the skeletons of an orangutan, chimpanzee, ape, gorilla, and a man, assuring us there is a definite pattern showing all have come from one common ancestor! This does not prove man has kept evolving over millions of years and that the ape or the chimpanzee was our ancestor. They have come up with various skeletons such as, the Piltdown man, which they said was proof that man came from monkeys, but they have been proven to be fakes. The similarity of the skeletons does not prove evolution, but it does prove that there is similarity in design. It shows that the same "architect" had the same general plan and design in mind. It shows functional similarity.

While we are able to breed and cultivate many new varieties, they are still of the same kind, and not species, of life. There is an absolute, irrefutable, immutable, unchangeable law, which absolutely prohibits a jump from one kind to another kind. There are hundreds of different varieties within a certain species, but they are the same species, dog, fish, birds, etc. The Bible tells us in Genesis 1:24-25 God said, "Let the earth bring forth the living creature according to his kind; cattle, and creeping things, and the beast of the earth according to his kind, and it was so. And God made the beast of the earth according to their kind, and cattle according to their kind, and everything that creeps upon the earth after his kind, and God saw that it was good."

This absolutely proves not only the existence of a lawgiver, but that there is alive, acting right now, a great sustainer of all that has been created. These laws are upheld, sustained, and kept in action by God. **Our God is the great sustainer!**

The total interdependency of all life forms, the tremendous design by one great Designer with an overall framework of a plan of creation into which all life forms fit, demands a sustainer. Nothing lives or dies to itself. Each living thing, whether plant or animal, when it dies, supplies life for other living things. Observe a forest. A tree grows, finally dies, and falls only to become part of the fallow forest floor, supplying life-giving elements for the young trees, which it had sown in its lifetime! Ask an evolutionist which evolved first, the corn or the bee? Did the bee evolve slowly for thousands of years, independent of the corn, the flowers, and the pollens from growing things which are his life source, or did the corn, flowers, and pollens gradually evolve for thousands of years independent of the little bee, upon which they must rely for their very continuation of life? Which came first, the chicken or the egg? We know that in the beginning was God! **Our God is the great originator!**

Look around you. Have you ever seen an ugly sunset, an ugly scene in the mountains, the desert, at sea, or anywhere on earth, unless man made it? All is in harmony! Look at the wings of a bird or a fly, the facets of a quartz crystal, or the masterpiece of all designs, the human body. All point out that for such intricate design, there had to be a great designer. **Our God is the great designer!**

Fulfilled Prophecy proves that God exists. One third of the Bible is prophecy and almost one-half of the prophecies were fulfilled when Jesus came to earth over two thousand years ago. Only an omniscient (all-knowing) God could foretell events before they happen. **Our God is omniscient!**

Answered Prayer is a divine, supernatural intervention, and direct answer from Almighty God! It is the result of being obedient to God's laws, asking according to His will, and then believing in faith until the answer comes. **Our God answers prayer!**

Changed lives are what you see before your very eyes when God takes a person who is so vile and wicked and changes them from the inside out into a warm and loving individual; this proves there is a God. A person cannot change himself nor can any other individual. Only **Our God changes lives!**

**Summary:**

- **Everything that happens is caused by existing laws. Our God is the Great Law Giver!**

- **Life can only come from life. Our God is the Great Life Giver!**

- **Matter had to be created. Our God is the Great Creator!**

- **Something sustains all the laws of the universe. Our God is the Great Sustainer!**

- **All life forms are interdependent of each other, so there had to be an origin at some point. Our God is the Great Originator!**

- **Look at the harmony of design. There had to be a designer. Our God is the Great Designer!**

- **Fulfilled prophecy demands someone who knows the beginning from the end. Our God is omniscient (or all knowing)!**

- **Answered prayer proves Our God answers prayer!**

- **A person can try all he wants to change himself but only Our God can change a person!**

Romans 1:19-20 "That which may be known of God is manifest (obvious) to them; for God has shown it to them. For the invisible things of Him from the creation of the world are clearly seen, being understood by the things that are made, even His eternal power and Godhead; so that they are without excuse."

The above scripture could not be clearer. All one has to do is look and think about everything around him, and he has to know there is a God. These proofs of the existence of God represent only the minutest beginning of the subject! Nevertheless, they are proofs. It is time for us to say with Job, "I know that my Redeemer lives, and that He shall stand at the latter day upon the earth."[7]

# Chapter 2

## IS THE BIBLE CREDIBLE FOR TODAY?

The Bible is not just another book, it is God's infallible (incapable of error, sure, certain), inerrant (free from error), word to mankind. If we can understand where the Bible originated, what it contains, who wrote it, and why it should be studied, we will begin to see what a wealth of information it contains. For those of us who have studied, applied, and obeyed its commands, we tell you implicitly: "Yes, the Bible can be believed and trusted. The truths found in its pages can bring you hope, love, joy, and greatest of all, peace to your soul, if you obey."

Someone has said the Holy Bible contains: the mind of God, the state of man, the way of salvation, the doom of sinners, and the happiness of believers. Its doctrines are holy, its precepts are binding; its histories are true, and its decisions are immutable. Read it to be wise, believe it to be safe, and practice it to be holy. It contains light to direct you, food to support you, and comfort to cheer you. It is the traveler's map, the pilgrim's staff, the pilot's compass, the soldier's sword, and the Christian's charter. In it paradise is restored, heaven opened, and the gates of Hell disclosed. Christ is its grand subject, our good its intent, and the glory of God its end. It should fill the memory, rule the heart, and guide the feet. Read it slowly, frequently, and prayerfully. It is a mine of wealth, a paradise of glory, and a river of pleasure. It is given to you in time, will be opened at judgment, and be remembered forever. It involves the highest responsibility, rewards the greatest labor, and condemns all who trifle with its holy contents.

The Bible says in Matthew 7:24-25 "Whosoever hears these sayings of mine, and doeth them, I will liken him unto a wise man, which built his house upon a rock; and the rain descended and the floods came, and the winds blew, and beat upon that house; and it fell not: for it was founded upon a rock." God's word is the rock on which the foundation of the Christian faith is built.

## Some of the names or phrases given to identify the Bible are:

| | |
|---|---|
| The Word of God | God's Plan for Man |
| Manufacturer's Handbook | God's Love Letter |
| The Book of Life | The Bread of Life |
| The Holy Scriptures | The Truth |
| The Inspired Word of God | God's Promises to Man |
| The Christian's Sword | |

What a person believes about the Bible is vital to their walk as a Christian. If they do not believe the Bible is the infallible, inerrant, Word of God, they have no foundation on which to build their Christian Life. It is not just a book! If it were, then any other book could be just as good. It is God's Word to and for His people. It is the Word of God. The Bible says Jesus is the Word. The more Word you get into your spirit, the more your spirit becomes like the Word, Jesus.

The name, Holy Bible, describes the book. Holy—means to be set apart from all that is sinful or impure; entirely free from impurity. Bible—is an English word which came originally from the name of papyrus, or the Byblos reed, used extensively in antiquity for making scrolls and books. Byblos was a Phoenician seaport and was so named because of the manufacture of papyrus writing material. Quite naturally, the Greek term for book was biblos, and a small book was called biblion. They called the sacred scripture "Ta Biblia" meaning "the books". When the title was translated from Greek to Latin, it was rendered in the singular and came into English as the word Bible. Thus, Bible means collection of books. There are 66 books in all. Each one is complete in itself, yet it takes all sixty-six to make a complete story.

Of these 66 books there are:

| | | |
|---|---|---|
| 39 Old Testament Books | 27 New Testaments Books | Totaling 66 |
| 5 Law | 4 Gospels | |
| 12 History | 1 History | |
| 5 Poetry | 14 Paul's Letters | |
| 5 Major Prophets | 7 General Letters | |
| 12 Minor Prophets | 1 Revelation | |

Catholic Bibles contain 11 of the 16 Books of the Apocrypha, which appeared in time between the Old and New Testaments. They came down in close connection with the books that were canonized. (Canonized means set apart as authentic.) The Jews of the Dispersion in Egypt had a high regard for these books and they were included in the Septuagint (an early translation of the Old Testament) but were rejected by the Jews of Palestine as not being inspired. The reasons Protestants reject their canonicity: Jesus never quoted anything from these books, and most of the early Fathers regarded them as uninspired.

The Bible contains every form of literature: biographies, letters, orations, prayers, and poems, stories of adventure, crime, mysteries, plots, drama, tender love lyrics, proverbs, epigrams, genealogies, and chronologies. The vigor and dramatic force have not been excelled in any other writing. As literature, it is said to have had a greater impression upon the human mind than any other book. One cannot consider himself well read unless he is thoroughly acquainted with the Bible.

Without the history of the Bible, we cannot know the reason for intelligent life or the existence of the human race. We would not know where we came from or where we are going. It is an account of _real_ people, who had _real_ problems, who found a _real_ solution in trusting and obeying God.

The Old Testament, or covenant, contains the covenant God made with Abraham. It also contains God's account of his creation of the world, His creation of man, the fall of man through sin and the history of one race of people, the Jews, who were blessed by God to be the race of people through whom the prophets foretold a savior would come to redeem mankind from the curse of sin.

The New Testament, or covenant, contains the covenant God made with us. It also contains the birth, life, death, burial, and resurrection of our savior, Jesus Christ. It tells us of his un-acceptance by his own people, the Jews. It brings hope to us, non-Jews, that were lost and without a savior. It tells us if we accept Jesus, the sacrifice that God has provided to save us from our sins, we can have eternal life. It teaches us how we can live a victorious life now and how we can look forward to His soon coming again when we will live with Him eternally.

People often say the "Old Testament is Christ concealed and the New Testament is Christ revealed." This refers to the fact that the Old Testament points to some unknown savior who is hidden from the people who lived in Old Testament times, and the New Testament reveals Jesus as the Savior of the World. Others refer to the Old and New Testaments as the Old and New Covenants which is not altogether accurate for the simple reason that the Mosaic Covenant and legal dispensation was in operation throughout the life, times and up until the death of Jesus, which includes the four gospels in the New Testament. When the veil of the temple was rent from the top to the bottom on the day Christ was crucified, it signified that a "new and living way" was opened for all believers to go into the very presence of God with no other sacrifice or priesthood necessary, except Jesus Christ. It was only as a result of the death, burial, and resurrection of Christ, the giving of the Holy Spirit at Pentecost, and the preaching of the gospel of grace that actually saw the outworking of the new covenant. The Old Testament traces the history of the Jewish people and the development of their faith in one God. The New Testament deals with the life, works, and teachings of Jesus Christ and his disciples.

Now we come to the question, "Who wrote the Bible?" We are told in the Bible it was written by the inspiration of the Holy Spirit. What do we mean by inspired? One writer said, "When I think of God inspiring writers; I think of a sailboat being driven by the wind." The prophets of old prophesied without knowing the fullness of what they were prophesying. So, also these men could write down what came from God as the Holy Spirit carried them in the desired direction. Except for a few isolated cases, God did not dictate His Word to the Bible writers. The writers were active in the process. They expressed their personal concerns. We read their prayers and observe differences in style and vocabulary. These factors add richness to the inspired Word that would be missing if the authors had merely acted as God's secretaries. To a world of uncertainty, God breathed out His Word so that we might have authoritative answers to the problems that confront us.

The Bible states in:

I Timothy 3:16-17 "All scripture is given by inspiration of God (God breathed) and is profitable for doctrine, for reproof, for correction, for instruction in righteousness that the man of God may be perfectly, thoroughly furnished unto all good works."

II Peter 1:20-21 "Knowing this first that no prophecy of the scriptures is of any private interpretation, for the prophecy came not in old times by the will of man, but holy men of God spoke as they were moved (carried along) by the Holy Spirit."

The Bible was written by 40 Different Men (all Jews except, perhaps Luke.) It was written over a period of 1400-1500 years. The writers were shepherds, kings, prophets, a tax collector, a tentmaker, a physician, a fisherman, and disciples of Jesus.

The Old Testament was written in the Hebrew language with the exception of a few sections that were written in Aramaic. The New Testament was written in Greek because of the immigration of the Jews to Greece after the temple and Jerusalem were destroyed in 70 A.D.

A good formula for remembering pertinent facts about the Bible: 66-40—1400-1500. Sixty-six different books, each having its own theme, and its own style. Written by forty different men over a period of 1400-1500 years, yet having a unified purpose that can be seen when the books come together. The Old Testament is incomplete in itself. It all points to a coming Messiah that will save the nation of Israel and the gentiles as well. The New Testament reveals Jesus as the long awaited redeemer, the Messiah of the Old Testament. The reader is aware that the continuity of the Bible must obviously be the work of one mind. Whose mind? **GOD'S.** His love runs through every book!

As previously stated, we would not know the reason for intelligent life, or existence of the human race, without the Bible. It tells where we came from and where we are going. The Bible tells us who God is, His account of creation of the world, and why the Jews are a special people. It foretells in the Old Testament who the Messiah would be and then it tells in the New Testament who He is. It tells us how we can be forgiven of our sins and receive eternal life. See the following examples.

**John 3:16-17** "For God so loved the world that He gave His only begotten Son, that whoever believes in Him should not perish but have everlasting life. God did not send His Son into the world to condemn the world, but that the world through Him might be saved."

**Romans 1:16-17** "For I am not ashamed of the gospel of Christ, for it is the power of God to salvation for everyone who believes, for the Jew first and also for the Greek. For in it the righteousness of God is revealed from faith to faith; as it is written, 'The just shall live by faith.'"

**James 1:21** "Therefore lay aside all filthiness and overflow of wickedness, and receive with meekness the implanted word, which is able to save your souls."

The Bible is one of the weapons of warfare we use to fight the devil. That is why it is called the sword of the spirit.

**Ephesians 6:10-17** "Finally, my brethren, be strong in the Lord and in the power of His might. Put on the whole armor of God that you may be able to stand against the wiles of the devil. We do not wrestle against flesh and blood, but against principalities, against powers, against the rulers of the darkness of this age, against spiritual hosts of wickedness in the heavenly places. Therefore take up the whole armor of God that you may be able to withstand in the evil day, and having done all, to stand. Stand therefore, having girded your waist with truth, having put on the breastplate of righteousness, and having shod your feet with the preparation of the gospel of peace; above all, taking the shield of faith with which you will be able to quench all the fiery darts of the wicked one. And take the helmet of salvation, and the sword of the Spirit, which is the word of God."

An education is not complete without knowledge of the Bible. Not only is the Bible the most widely circulated and influential book of human history, it is the most important influence in our Western civilization. There are repeated references to the Bible in the world's great literature, not only English and American, but also Russian and French literature as well. The history of Europe and of America cannot be understood without knowing how the Bible influenced it. Law and the basic ideals of democracy owe their largest debt to the Bible. A person cannot even be an intelligent and honest skeptic until he knows what he is rejecting.

The Bible gives us our belief system, it convicts of sin, if obeyed it corrects our behavior, and it instructs us in righteousness.

**2 Timothy 3:16** "All Scripture is given by inspiration of God, and is profitable for doctrine, for reproof, for correction, for instruction in righteousness."

Faith in God comes from hearing the Word of God.

**Romans 10:14** How then shall they call on Him in whom they have not believed? And how shall they believe in Him of whom they have not heard? And how shall they hear without a preacher? And how shall they preach unless they are sent? As it is written: "How beautiful are the feet of those who preach the gospel of peace, who bring glad tidings of good things!" But they have not all obeyed the gospel. Isaiah says, "Lord who has believed our report?" Faith comes by hearing, and hearing by the word of God.

Without the Bible, we would not know Jesus.

**1 Corinthians 15:1** Moreover, brethren, I declare to you the gospel which I preached to you, which also you received and in which you stand, by which also you are saved, if you hold fast that word which I preached to you—unless you believed in vain. For I delivered to you first of all that which I also received: that Christ died for our sins according to the Scriptures, and that He was buried, and that He rose again the third day according to the Scriptures, and that He was seen by Cephas, then by the twelve. After that He was seen by over five hundred brethren at once, of whom the greater part remain to the present, but some have fallen asleep. After that He was seen by James, then by all the apostles. Then last of all He was seen by me also, as by one born out of due time.

The Scriptures build us up and give us an inheritance.

**Acts 20:32** "So now, brethren, I commend you to God and to the word of His grace, which is able to build you up and give you an inheritance among all those who are sanctified.

**2 Timothy 3:17** That the man of God may be perfect, thoroughly equipped for every good work.

The Bible is not just some book to lie on a table to collect dust. It is free from error. It is a sure word defining faith, doctrines, and morals; a road map for the Christian life! "Read it to be wise, believe it to be safe, and practice it to be right."

Someone has said: "Did you know that when you carry the Bible Satan has a headache; when you open it, he collapses, when he sees you reading it, he loses his strength, and when you stand on the Word of God, Satan can't hurt you!"

# Chapter 3

## DO CHRISTIANS BELIEVE IN THREE GODS?

M any people think Christians believe in more than one God because we believe in the concept of the Trinity. Our belief in the Trinity needs to be understood as it is one of the most profound and important doctrines in the Bible.

I have heard there are more mainline Christians lured into cults than any other group of people. Someone puts doubt in their belief system by telling them the word "Trinity" is not found in the Bible. Most cults say the word trinity cannot be found in the Bible; they say the doctrine of the trinity is not rational, cannot be understood, and that it originated with Satan. Many deny the Deity of Jesus. Jesus is undermined when men proclaim He was just a good man, a prophet, or a good teacher. He is who He said He is or He is the greatest hoax that has ever been perpetrated on mankind. Some say Jesus was the first creation of God that died and came back an invisible spirit. Some say He is the archangel Michael. Others say He and Lucifer were brothers. Many refer to the personality of the Holy Spirit as "it." Others say the Holy Spirit is an impersonal force. Because they have no foundational beliefs they doubt what they have been told by their denomination.

If we know the truth about the Doctrine of the Trinity, where it originated, and why we believe what we do based on God's Word, then we will be armed for battle when someone tells us that the word trinity is not found in the Bible, and it was a lie made up by Satan.

It is true the word trinity is not in the Bible. The concept is more implied rather than explained. There is only one God, one divine nature, and one being. This divine being is tri-personal, involving the distinction of the Father, the Son, and the Holy Spirit. These three are joint partakers of the same nature and majesty of God.

When early Christian believers began to openly acknowledge Jesus Christ as the Son of God and to recognize the Holy Spirit as the indwelling presence of God, many Jews accused them of violating the worship of one God. The most sacred scripture for the Jews is found in Deuteronomy 6:4 "Hear, O Israel: The Lord our God, the Lord is one." They said Christians worshipped more than one God. Since the early church was concentrating more on evangelism and survival than on theology, they allowed several centuries to pass before expressing a clear doctrine of the Trinity.

The crucial turning point for the debate concerning the Trinity came when the Roman Emperor Constantine convened a council of the church at the city of Nicea in A.D. 325. Arius and Athanasius held the two main opposing views, both of whom were church officials from Alexandria, Egypt.

Arius maintained that there is only one God who had no beginning, and that God created the Son out of nothing, before He made the world. The Son thus became the greatest and first of all created beings, but was different and apart from God the Father.

Athanasius contended that the Son is eternally generated by God the Father and is of the same essence as the Father. Although there is no division in God's essential being, the Son is a distinct Person.

Constantine sided with Athanasius, and the Council of Nicea produced a bedrock statement concerning the Trinity. It begins: "We believe in one God, Father Almighty, maker of all things visible and invisible; and in one Lord Jesus Christ the Son of God, begotten of the Father, only begotten that is from the substance of the Father." Near the bottom of the creed, the council added the brief statement, "And we believe in the Holy Spirit."

Fifty-six years later, the church's Council of Constantinople stated more fully that the Father, Son, and Holy Spirit constitute one Godhead, existing simultaneously in three modes of being. Within the nature of the one God, there are three eternal persons: Father, Son and Holy Spirit. At this point I would like for you to see the Holy Spirit is a person, not a force as some say.

There are fourteen different ways to say "one" in the Hebrew Language. The following are two ways I would like to mention:

Echad—means two or more and is a plural word.

Gebur—means one and is a singular word.

Deuteronomy 6:4 "Hear oh Israel the Lord our God is one God." Here the word Echad is used which means that God is plural in this passage. Elohim, the plural (more than one) Hebrew name for God, is used approximately five hundred times in the first five books of the Bible, followed consistently by a singular verb. (I.e. Gen. 1:26, 27; 3:22; 11:7) Many scholars believe that Elohim reveals the oneness of God, as well as a plurality of Persons in the Godhead.

The Spirit of God is referred to early in the Book of Genesis, as well as many other places in the Old Testament. God is distinguished from the Holy Spirit in Psalms 104:30, where God is described as sending forth His Spirit. We must acknowledge the Holy Spirit is a person from what we learn in the Bible. The Bible quotes the Holy Spirit as <u>saying</u> something in Acts 13:2. A force cannot talk. In Acts 5:3 "Ananias, how is it that Satan has so filled your heart that you have <u>lied</u> to the Holy Spirit? You have not lied to men but to God." You cannot lie to a force. In Ephesians 4:30 we discover He can be <u>grieved.</u> You can't grieve a force, only a person.

As you can see from these few verses, and there are countless others, the characteristics attributed to the Holy Spirit confirm that He is a person.

## NEW TESTAMENT REVELATIONS OF THE TRINITY:

If I can show you that there are three persons in the New Testament each called God, and that there is only one Jehovah God, would you not agree that the three are the same God?

- **The Father is Jehovah God**

II Peter 1:17 "For Jesus received from God the Father honor and glory when such a voice came to Him from the Excellent Glory: 'This is my beloved Son, in whom I am well pleased.'"

- **Jesus the Son and God the Father are both referred to as the Alpha and the Omega, the first and the last.**

Revelation 1:8 Jesus says, "I am the Alpha and the Omega, the beginning and the end. Who is, and who was, and who is to come, the Almighty." God the Father identifies Himself as the Almighty God but here Jesus says He is the Almighty.

Revelation 1:17-18 "Do not be afraid. I am the First and the Last. I am the Living One; I was dead, and behold I am alive forever and ever!" Who died? Jesus was the one who died and here is saying He is the beginning and the end.

Revelation 21:5 "He who was seated on the throne said, 'I am making everything new! It is done. I am the Alpha and the Omega, the Beginning and the End.'" Who is sitting on the throne? God the Father, and He says He is the beginning and the end.

Revelation 22:12 **"Behold I am coming quickly and my reward is with me, to give to every one according to his word. I am the Alpha and the Omega, the Beginning and the End, the First and the Last."** Who is speaking? Jesus the Son identifies himself as the beginning and the end.

Isaiah 7:14 "Therefore the Lord himself will give you a sign: Behold, the virgin shall conceive and bear a Son, and shall call His name Immanuel." Immanuel means God with us. We understand this is speaking of Jesus the Son but it says God is with us.

Isaiah 44:6 "This is what the Lord says—Israel's King and Redeemer, the Lord Almighty: I am the first and I am the last; apart from me there is no God."

In these scriptures God the Father and God the Son both claim to be the Alpha and Omega, the first and the last.

- **God and Jesus both refer to themselves as I AM.**

Exodus 3:13-14 Moses said to God, "Suppose I go to the Israelites and say to them "The God of your fathers has sent me to you, and they ask me, "What is his name?" Then what shall I tell them?" God said to Moses, "I AM WHO I AM". This is what you are to say to the Israelites: "I AM has sent me to you."

John 8:56-58 **"Your father Abraham rejoiced at the thought of seeing my day, he saw it and was glad. You (Jesus) are not yet 50 years old the Jews said to him, and you have seen Abraham? "I tell you the truth, before Abraham was born, I AM."**

- **Jesus says He and God are one and the same.**

John 14:6-10 Jesus said unto him, "I am the way, the truth, and the life. No man cometh unto the Father except through Me. If ye had known Me you would have known My Father also: and from now on you know Him and have seen Him." Philip said unto him, "Lord show us the Father, and it is sufficient for us." Jesus said to him, "Have I been with you so long, and yet you have not known Me? He who has seen Me has seen the Father; so how can you say, 'Show us the Father'?

## THE BIBLE SAYS:

- **God created the heavens and Earth.**

Genesis 1:1 "In the beginning God (plural in meaning) created the heavens and the earth." If the word is plural, you have to ask, "Who else was there?"

Genesis 1:26 Then God said, "Let Us make man in Our image, according to Our likeness." Whose image and whose likeness?

- **The Word created all things.**

John 1:1 "In the beginning was the Word, and the Word was with God, and the Word was God. He was with God in the beginning. Through him all things were made; without him nothing was made that has been made. In Him was life, and that life was the light of men."

John 1:14 "And the Word became flesh and dwelt among us, and we beheld His glory, the glory of the only begotten of the Father, full of grace and truth. Jesus is the Word, so we know Jesus was in the beginning."

- **The Spirit was at creation.**

Genesis 1:2 "And the Spirit of God was hovering over the face of the waters."

## THE HOLY SCRIPTURES WERE WRITTEN BY:

- **God:** 2 Timothy 3:16 "All scripture is God-breathed."

- **Holy Spirit:** 2 Peter 1:20 "Men spoke from God as they were carried along by the Holy Spirit."

- **Jesus Christ:** Galatians 1:11-12 "The gospel I preached is not something that man made up, I did not receive it from any man, nor was I taught it; rather, I received it by revelation from Jesus Christ."

## OUR BODY IS THE TEMPLE OF GOD And ALSO THE TEMPLE OF THE HOLY SPIRIT:

- 1 Corinthians 3:16-17 Don't you know that you yourselves are **God's temple** and that God's Spirit lives in you? If anyone destroys **God's temple**, God will destroy him.

- 1 Corinthians 6:19 Do you not know that your body is a **temple of the Holy Spirit?**

## ALL THREE APPEAR AS ONE IN THE FOLLOWING VERSES:

**The three were present at Jesus' conception.**

Luke 1:35 The Angel answered, "The Holy Spirit will come upon you, and the power of the Most High will overshadow you. So the Holy One to be born will be called the Son of God."

**The three were present at Jesus' baptism.**

Matthew 4:16-17 The heavens were opened to Him, and He saw the Spirit of God descending like a dove and alighting upon Him. And suddenly a voice came from heaven, saying, "This is My beloved Son, in whom I am well pleased."

**We are baptized into the three persons of the Trinity:** The Father, Son, and Holy Ghost.

Matthew 28:19 Go and make disciples of all nations, baptizing them in the name of the Father and of the Son and of the Holy Spirit".

We can conclude that God the Father is the original source of all things. God the Son was God's way of manifesting Himself to mankind and came as the embodiment of divine love and grace. God the Holy Spirit, the final revelation of God, bestows the blessings of the Father and the Son upon His children. The Holy Spirit convicts the world of sin, helps the believer understand God's word and shows him the way of righteousness, and seals those who are redeemed by God's grace.

While we will never fully comprehend the mystery and unity of the Trinity, we give equal reverence, love, and obedience to the Father, Son, and the Holy Spirit.

With our finite minds it is hard to understand the mystery of the Doctrine of the Trinity. However, I trust from the information I have given you that you will be able to see that the attributes of the Father, Son, and the Holy Spirit all point to one being made in three distinct personalities and functions called the Trinity.

# Chapter 4

## WHO IS GOD THE FATHER?

The basis of Christianity is built on the life, teachings, death, and resurrection of Jesus Christ. It is belief in what Jesus has done for mankind that Christians are redeemed from a life of sin and receive eternal life. Sometimes the question of "Who is God the Father?" seems obscure. As we delve into this question and find answers, you should have a deeper appreciation and love for God. As we understand His nature and His characteristics, our faith should increase and hearts should be encouraged. When we understand who He is, it makes sin look foolish and righteousness look excellent. It makes persevering in hardship seem reasonable, and it produces in our spirit a big "yes" response to obeying a call to do the will of God. The devil knows if he can blind our understanding to what God is like, he has then leveraged the battle significantly in his favor. There is nothing that awakens our hearts with motivation to whole hearted love as when God reveals himself to us.

In our study "Do Christians Believe in Three Gods?" we discovered there is one Being made in three distinct personalities and functions called the Trinity. The Old Testament reveals God the Father, the New Testament reveals God the Son, and the book of Acts reveals God the Holy Ghost. As we read in the Old Testament of God's dealing with the descendants of Abraham, Isaac and Jacob, His attributes are revealed. Most of us have read the stories in the Old Testament, but today we want to think about what God has revealed about Himself through those stories. Every act of God builds on the past with a view toward the future.

## God is described as the Lord Almighty

Genesis 17:1 And when Abram was ninety years old and nine, the Lord appeared to Abram, and said unto him, I am the Almighty God; walk before me, and be thou perfect.

Revelation 1:8 I am Alpha and Omega, the beginning and the ending, saith the Lord, which is, and which was, and which is to come, the Almighty.

## God is described as the creator

Genesis 1:1 In the beginning God created the heavens and the earth.

Nehemiah 9:6 You alone are the Lord. You made the heavens, even the highest heavens and all their starry host, the earth and all that is on it, the seas and all that is in them. You give life to everything, and the multitudes of heaven worship you.

Psalms 102:25 In the beginning You laid the foundations of the earth, and the heavens are the work of Your hands.

Since God made everything including you and me, doesn't it make sense when we have a problem that He can solve any problem that we take to Him?

## God is described as the Father

Matthew 28:19 Go ye therefore, and teach all nations, baptizing them in the Name of the Father, and of the Son, and of the Holy Ghost.

1 Corinthians 8:6 But to us there is but one God, the Father, of whom are all things, and we in Him and one Lord Jesus Christ, by whom are all things, and we by Him.

2 Corinthians 15:24 Then the end comes, when He shall have delivered up the kingdom to God even the Father, when He shall have put down all rule, and all authority and power.

## God is described as King

Psalms 10:16 "The LORD is King forever and ever: the heathen are perished out of his land."

Psalms 24:7-10 **"Lift up your heads, O you gates,**

And be lifted up, you everlasting doors!

And the King of glory shall come in.

Who is this King of glory?

The LORD strong and mighty,

The LORD mighty in battle.

Lift up your heads, O you gates!

Lift up, you everlasting doors!

And the King of glory shall come in.

Who is this King of glory?

The LORD of hosts,

He is the King of glory."

1st Timothy 1:17 "Now unto the King eternal, immortal, invisible, the only wise God, be honor and glory for ever and ever. Amen."

## WHAT DOES GOD SAY ABOUT HIMSELF?

Genesis 17:1 "When Abraham was 93 years old the Lord appeared to him and said, "I Am God Almighty".

Exodus 3:14 "God said to Moses, 'I Am that I Am': that shall you say unto the children of Israel, I Am has sent me unto you."

**I Am!** God is who He is. The absolute I. The self-existent one. God is everything. He is not in everything as the Pantheists and New Agers say; He is everything, without Him there would be nothing. He has always been, He always is, and He will always be.

Exodus 3:5 "God spoke to Moses from the midst of the burning bush and said, "Draw not nigh hither: put off thy shoes from off your feet, for the place where on you stand is holy ground. More over He said. I Am the God thy father, the God of Abraham, the

God of Isaac and the God of Jacob (vs. 15) this is my name forever. Moses hid his face; for he was afraid to look upon God."

## WHAT ARE GOD'S ATTRIBUTES?

### He is eternal

Genesis 21:33 "And Abraham planted a grove in Beer-Sheba, and called there on the name of the Lord, the everlasting God."

Jeremiah 10:10 "But the Lord is the true God, he is the living God; and an everlasting King: at his wrath the earth shall tremble, and the nations shall not be able to abide his indignation."

1 Timothy 6:15 "Which in His times He shall show, who is the blessed and only Potentate, the Kings of kings, and the Lord of lords; Who only hath immortality, dwelling in the light which no man can approach unto; whom no man hath seen, nor can see: to whom be honor and power everlasting."

### God is immutable (cannot change)

Numbers 23: 19 "God is not a man that He should lie; neither the son of man that He should repent: hath He said, and shall He not do it? Or hath he spoken and shall he not make it good?"

Psalms 119: 80 "Forever, O Lord, the word is settled in heaven."

Micah 3:6 "I am the Lord, I change not."

James 1:7 "Every good gift and every perfect gift is from above, and cometh down from the Father of lights, with whom is no variableness, neither shadow of turning."

### God is omnipresent

This means that God is free from the laws or limits of space. He is present at all places at all times; an attribute of God alone.

Psalms 139:7-11 "Where can I go from Your Spirit? Or where can I flee from Your presence? If I ascend into heaven, You are there. If I make my bed in hell, behold, You are there. If I take the wings of the morning, and dwell in the uttermost parts of the sea, even there Your hand shall lead me, and Your right hand shall hold me. If I say, surely the darkness shall fall on me—indeed the darkness shall not hide from You."

Proverbs 15:3 "The eyes of the Lord are in every place, keeping watch on the evil and the good."

Jeremiah 23:23-24 "Am I a God near at hand, says the Lord, and not a God afar off? Can anyone hide himself in secret places, so I shall not see him? Says the Lord; Do I not fill heaven and earth?"

## God is omnipotent

He has all power, unlimited authority and influence.

Job 42:2 "I know that You can do all things; no plan of Yours can be thwarted."

Psalms 115:3 "Our God is in heaven; He does whatever pleases Him."

Romans 9:20 "What are you, O man, to talk back to God? Shall what is formed say to him who formed it, why did you make me like this? Does not the potter have the right to make out of the same lump clay some pottery for noble purposes and some for common use?"

## God is omniscient (All knowing)

He has infinite awareness, understanding and insight. He possesses universal or complete knowledge.

Job 31:4 "Does He not see my ways and count my every step?"

Hebrews 4:12-13 "The word of God is living and active, sharper than a double-edged sword. It penetrates even to dividing soul and spirit, joints and marrow; it judges the thoughts and attitudes of the heart. Nothing in all creation is hidden from God's sight. Everything is uncovered and laid bare before the eyes of Him to whom we must give account." His directions for my life are right.

## He is divine perfection

Deuteronomy 32:4 "He is the Rock, His works are perfect, and all His ways are just. A faithful God who does no wrong, upright and just is He."

## Man is made in His image

Genesis 1:27 "God created man in His own image, in the image of God He created him; male and female He created them."

John 4:24 "God is a spirit: and they that worship Him must worship Him in spirit and in truth."

# WHAT IS GOD'S NATURE?

## God is Love

1 John 4:8 "He that loves not knows not God for God is love."

Jeremiah 31:3 "The Lord appeared to us in the past, saying, "I have loved you with an everlasting love; I have drawn you with loving kindness."

John 3:16 "For God so loved the world that He gave His one and only son, that whoever believes in Him shall not perish but have eternal life."

Romans 5:8 "God demonstrates His own love for us in this: While we were yet sinners, Christ died for us."

Ephesians 2:4-5 "Because of His great love for us, God, who is rich in mercy made us alive with Christ even when we were dead in transgressions—it is by grace you are saved."

We are loved by God! The Creator of this universe, the God who made Adam and Eve, the God who designed this wonderful planet on which we live, the sun, the moon, and the stars. He loved you and me so much that even though we were so unworthy of His great love and mercy, He sent His only son to die for me and for you while we were still sinners, so that we could have eternal life. Imagine God loves us! We should never feel unloved or insignificant ever again. He validates us as special! That's something to get excited about!

## God is Merciful

Micah 7:18 "Who is a God like You, who pardons sin and forgives the transgression of the remnant of his inheritance? You do not stay angry forever but delight to show mercy."

Titus 3:5 "He saved us, not because of righteous things we had done, but because of His mercy, He saves us through the washing of rebirth and renewal by the Holy Spirit."

## God is Peace

Ephesians 2:14 "He is our peace . . ."

2 Thessalonians 3:16 "Now the Lord of Peace Himself give you peace always by all means. The Lord be with you."

Hebrews 13:20 "Now the God of peace that brought again from the dead our Lord Jesus, that great shepherd of the sheep through the blood of the everlasting covenant."

## God Is Faithful

Deuteronomy 7:9 "Know that the Lord your God is God; He is the faithful God, keeping his covenant of love to a thousand generations of those who love Him and keep His commands."

1 Kings 8:56 "Not one word has failed of all the good promises He gave through His servant Moses."

Psalms 108:4 "For great is Your love, higher than the heavens Your faithfulness reaches to the skies."

## God Is Good

Psalms 33:5 "The Lord loves righteousness and justice; the earth is full of His unfailing love."

## God Is Gracious

Psalms 84:11 "The Lord God is a sun and shield; the Lord bestows favor and honor; no good thing does He withhold from those whose walk is blameless."

## God is impartial

Job 34:18-19 "Is He not the One who says to kings, 'You are worthless:' and to nobles, 'You are wicked, who shows no partiality to princes and does not favor the rich over the poor, for they are all the work of His hands?'"

Matthew 5:45 "He causes His sun to rise on the evil and the good, and sends rain on the righteous and the unrighteousness."

## God is just

Romans 2:2 "We know that God's judgment is based on truth."

## God is light

Psalms 27:1 "The Lord is my light and my salvation."

John 8:12 "Jesus spoke to them again, saying, 'I am the light of the world. He who follows Me shall not walk in darkness, but have the light of life.'"

1 John 1:5 "This is the message which we have heard from Him and declare to you, that God is light and in Him is no darkness at all."

## God is living

Acts 1:3 "He showed himself alive after His passion by many infallible proofs, being seen of them forty days and speaking of the things pertaining to the kingdom of God."

Revelation 1:18 "I am He that lived, and was dead; and behold, I am alive for evermore. Amen!"

## God is the God of Holiness
## (sacred, set apart, pure, clean, and blameless)

Exodus 15:11 "Who among the gods is like You, O Lord? Who is like You, majestic in holiness, awesome in glory, working wonders?"

1 Samuel 6:20 "The men asked, 'Who can stand in the presence of the Lord this holy God? To whom will the ark go up from here?'"

Isaiah 6:3 "They were calling to one another: "Holy, Holy, Holy is the Lord Almighty; the whole earth is full of His glory."

Hebrews 12:14 "Make every effort to live in peace with all men and be holy; without holiness no one will see the Lord.

Exodus 28:31, 33, 35 "The Lord said unto Moses: make the robe of the ephod all of blue. Upon the robe, you shall make pomegranates of blue and purple and scarlet yarn all around its hem, and bells of gold between them all around. Aaron must wear it when he ministers. The sound of the bells will be heard when he enters the Holy Place before the Lord and when he comes out, so he will not die."

Leviticus 19:1-2 "The Lord said to Moses, speak to the entire assembly of God and say to them: Be Holy because I, the Lord your God, am holy." Since God is holy, we are to be holy.

We choose to obey Him as we lead lives separated from all that is sinful, impure or morally wrong, and inwardly dedicate ourselves to God. He then gives us the grace to do the right thing, and He sets us apart from the world.

## He is the God of Truth

Numbers 23:19 "God is not a man that He should lie; neither the son of man that He should repent: hath He said, and shall He not do it? Or hath He spoken, and shall He not make it good?"

Hebrews 6:18 "God did this so that, by two unchangeable things in which it is impossible for God to lie, we who have fled to take hold of the hope offered to us may be greatly encouraged."

## He is the God of Righteousness.

Psalms 119:137 "Righteous are You, O Lord, and Your laws are right."

Psalms 145:17 "The Lord is righteous in all His ways and loving toward all He has made."

Psalms 97:2 "Clouds and thick darkness surround Him; righteousness and justice are the foundation of his throne."

## He is the God of Excellence

Isaiah 28:29 "All this comes from the Lord Almighty, wonderful in counsel and magnificent in wisdom."

The god that created this great universe, the Lord God Almighty is our Father God. The King of Kings and Lord of Lords, the great I AM is everything you will ever need Him to be. He is eternal, will never change, cannot lie, He is everywhere, He knows everything we think or do, He has all power and authority to do what He wants to do. Everything He does is perfect and He has made us in His image!

Our excellent, holy, righteous, God of truth, the god who loves us like a father, allows us to come boldly into the throne room to ask for grace and mercy in the time of need. He is loving, merciful, faithful, good, gracious, impartial, and just. He will give us peace because He is the God of Peace. Enjoy the following tribute to my God.

### "MY KING"

The Bible says my king is a seven way king:
He is the King of the Jews, that's a racial king.
He is the King of Israel, that's a national king.
He is the King of Righteousness.
He is the King of the Ages.
He is the King of Heaven.
He is the King of Glory.
He is the King of Kings and He is the Lord of Lords
That's My King!
Well—I wonder do you know Him?

David said the heavens declare the glory of God
and the firmament showeth His handiwork
My King is a sovereign King
No means of measure can define His limitless love.
No far-seeing telescope can bring into visibility the coastline
of His storeless supply.
No barrier can hinder Him from pouring out His blessings.
He's enduringly strong.
He's entirely sincere.
He's eternally steadfast.
He's immortally graceful.
He's imperially powerful.
He's impartially merciful.
Do you know Him?

He's the greatest phenomenon that has ever crossed the
Horizon of the world.
He's God's son.
He's the sinner's savior.
He's the centerpiece of civilization.
He stands in the solitude of Himself.
He's august and He's unique.
He's unparalleled
He's unprecedented.
He is the loftiest idea in literature.
He is the highest personality in philosophy.
He is the supreme problem in high criticism.
He is the fundamental doctrine of true theology.
He is the cause for the necessity for spiritual religion.
He is the miracle of the ages.
He is! Yes, He is!

He is the superlative of everything good that you choose
To call him.
He is the only one qualified to be an all sufficient savior.
I wonder if you know Him today.
He is the prize strength for the weak.
He is available for the tempted and the tried.
He sympathizes and He saves.

He is present and He sustains.
He guards and He guides.
He heals the sick.
He cleanses the leper.
He forgives the sinner.
He discharges debtors.
He delivers the captive.
He defends the feeble
He blesses the young.
He serves the unfortunate.
He regards the aged.
He rewards the diligent
And He beautifies the meek.
I wonder if you know Him.

Well, this is my King! He is the King!

He is the key to knowledge.
He is the well-spring of wisdom
He is the doorway of deliverance.
He is the pathway of peace.
He is the roadway of righteousness.
He is the highway of holiness.
He is the gateway of Glory.
Do you know Him?

Well—
His office is manifold.
His promise is sure.
His life is matchless.
His goodness is limitless.
His mercy is everlasting.
His love never changes.
His word is enough.
His grace is sufficient.
His reign is righteous.
His yoke is easy and His burdens light.
I wish I could describe Him to you—
But He is indescribable!

Yes He Is.

This God he's . . . .
He's incomprehensible.
He's invincible.
He's irresistible.
Well, you can't get Him out of your mind!
Well, you can't get him off your hands.
Well, you can't out live Him
And you can't live without Him!
The Pharisees couldn't stand Him
But they found out they couldn't stop Him!
Pilate couldn't find any fault in Him!
The witnesses couldn't get their testimonies to agree!
Herod couldn't kill Him!
Death couldn't handle Him!
And the grave couldn't hold Him!
Yeah—That's my King—That's my King!

And thine is the Kingdom and the power and the glory
Forever and ever and ever and ever.
How long is that?
And ever and ever and ever and when you get through all of the
Forevers—then AMEN!
This God of mine!—Amen!—Amen!

7 Minute Sermon by S.M. Lockridge

# Chapter 5

## IS JESUS THE JEWISH MESSIAH?

The most amazing drama that has ever been presented to the mind of man, a drama written in prophecy in the Old Testament and in the biography of the Gospels, is the narrative of Jesus Christ. One outstanding fact, among many, completely isolates Him. He is the only Man in the history of the world that had explicit details given beforehand of His birth, life, death, and resurrection. These details are in documents given to the public centuries before He appeared. This is a fact that no one challenges, or can challenge. These documents were widely circulated long before His birth, and anyone and everyone (the average Bible reader) can compare for himself the actual records of His life with those old documents and find that they match up perfectly. Probably you have heard the expression, "The Old Testament is in the New Testament revealed, and the New Testament is in the Old concealed". That simply means the Old Testament hid who the Messiah was going to be, and the New Testament reveals who He is.

The New Testament shows absolute proof that Jesus of Nazareth perfectly and completely fulfilled all the Old Testament predictions of the hope for a soon coming King. The personal deliverer for the nation of Israel is indeed the Messiah, the Savior of the world, the Son of the Living God.

As we study the prophecies of the Old Testament and see them revealed in the coming of the Lord Jesus, we will have an even clearer understanding that the whole of Scripture is an unfolding of God's Plan for mankind from the creation of the world. In addition it will further underline these facts:

- The Bible is the inspired Word of God, unaided man is neither capable of writing nor fulfilling such a literary wonder.

- The God of the Bible is the only One who knows the end from the beginning, and He alone has the power to fulfill all His Word, the true and living God.

- Demonstrate that the God of the Bible is both all-knowing to be able to foretell the future through numberless men and all-powerful to be able to bring to pass a perfect fulfillment of His Word in the midst of widespread unbelief, ignorance, and rebellion on the part of men.

## FULFILLED PROPHECY PROVES JESUS CHRIST OF THE NEW TESTAMENT IS THE JEWISH MESSIAH OF THE OLD TESTAMENT

Atheists and other skeptics try to deny the fulfillment of prophecy by saying they were accidental, chance, or co-incidental. Dr. Olinthus Gregory said, "Suppose there were only 50 prophecies in the Old Testament instead of 333. The probability of chance fulfillment as calculated by mathematicians according to the theory of probabilities is less than one in 1,125,000,000,000,000. Now add only two more prophecies, the time, and place at which they must happen, and the immense improbability that they will take place by chance exceeds all the power of numbers to express (or the mind of man to grasp).

There were 333 prophecies fulfilled at Jesus' first coming. Let us briefly trace a few of the outstanding points in the comparison of Old Testament prophecies and New Testament fulfillment.

The work of redemption was to be accomplished by one Person, the central figure in both testaments, the promised Messiah. Listed below is a brief summary of the prophecies given in the Old Testament (O.T.) and the fulfillment in the New Testament (N.T.)

As the "Seed of Woman" He was to bruise Satan's Head.

O.T. Genesis 3: 15 "And I will put enmity between thee and the woman, and between thy seed and her seed; it shall bruise thy head, and thou shall bruise his heel."

N.T. Galatians 4:4 "But when the fullness of the time was come, God sent forth his Son, made of a woman, made under the law."

As the "Seed of Abraham"

O.T. Genesis 22:18 "And in thy seed shall all the nations of the earth be blessed; because thou hast obeyed my voice."

N.T. Galatians 3:16 "Now to Abraham and his seed were the promises made. He said not and to seeds, as of many; but as of one, and to thy seed, which is Christ."

## As the "Seed of David"

O.T. Psalms 132:11 "The LORD hath sworn in truth unto David; He will not turn from it; of the fruit of thy body will I set upon thy throne". Behold, the days come, said the LORD, that I will raise unto David a righteous Branch, and a King shall reign and prosper, and shall execute judgment and justice in the earth.

N.T. Romans 1:3 "Concerning His Son Jesus Christ our Lord, who was born of the seed of David according to the flesh.

## He was to come from the tribe of Judah

O.T. Genesis 49:10 "The scepter shall not depart from Judah, nor a lawgiver from between his feet, until Shiloh come; and unto him shall the gathering of the people be."

N.T. Hebrews 7:14 "For it is evident that our Lord sprang out of Judah; of which tribe Moses spoke nothing concerning priesthood."

## He must come at a specified time

O.T. Daniel 9:24 "Seventy weeks are determined upon thy people and upon thy holy city, to finish the transgression, and to make an end of sins, and to make reconciliation for iniquity, and to bring in everlasting righteousness, and to seal up the vision and prophecy, and to anoint the most Holy."

N.T. John 4:25 "I know that Messiah is coming" (who is called Christ) "When He comes, He will tell us all things. Jesus said to her, "I who speak to you am He."

## He must be born of a virgin

O.T. Isaiah 7:14 "Therefore the Lord himself shall give you a sign; Behold a virgin shall conceive, and bear a son, and shall call his name Immanuel."

N.T. Matthew 1:18-23 "Now the birth of Jesus Christ was on this wise: When as his mother Mary was espoused to Joseph, before they came together; she was found with child of the Holy Ghost. Then Joseph her husband, being a just man, and not wanting to make her a public example, was minded to put her away secretly. But while he thought about these things, behold, an angel of the Lord appeared to him in a dream, saying, "Joseph, son of David, do not be afraid to take to you Mary your wife, for that which is conceived in her is of the Holy Spirit. And she will bring forth a Son, and you shall call His name JESUS, for He will save His people from their sins." Now all this was done that it might be fulfilled which was spoken by the Lord through the prophet, saying: "Behold, a virgin shall be with child, and bear a Son, and they shall call His name Immanuel," which is translated, "God with us."

## He was to be born in Bethlehem of Judea

O.T. Micah 5:2 "But you, Bethlehem Ephrathah, though you are little among the thousands of Judah, Yet out of you shall come forth to Me The One to be Ruler in Israel, Whose goings forth are from of old, from everlasting."

N.T. Matthew 2:6 "But you, Bethlehem, in the land of Judah, are not the least among the rulers of Judah, for out of you shall come a ruler, who will shepherd My people Israel."

## Great persons were to visit and adore Him

O.T. Psalms 72:10 "The kings of Tarshish and of the isles shall bring presents: the kings of Sheba and Seba shall offer gifts."

N.T. Matthew 2:1 "Wise men from the East came to Jerusalem, saying, "Where is He who has been born King of the Jews? For we have seen His star in the East and have come to worship Him."

## Through the rage of a jealous king innocent children were to be slaughtered

O.T. Jeremiah 31:15 "Thus says the LORD: "A voice was heard in Ramah, lamentation and bitter weeping, Rachel weeping for her children, refusing to be comforted for her children, because they *are* no more."

N.T. Matthew 2:16-18 "Then Herod, when he saw that he was deceived by the wise men, was exceedingly angry; and he sent forth and put to death all the male children who were in Bethlehem and in all its districts, from two years old and under, according to the time which he had determined from the wise men. Then was fulfilled what was spoken by Jeremiah the prophet, saying: "A voice was heard in Ramah, Lamentation, weeping, and great mourning, Rachel weeping for her children, refusing to be comforted, because they are no more."

## He was to be proceeded by a forerunner, John the Baptist, before entering his public ministry

O.T. Isaiah 40:3 "The voice of one crying in the wilderness: "Prepare the way of the LORD; Make straight in the desert, a highway for our God."

N.T. Luke 1:17 **"He will also go before Him in the spirit and power** of Elijah, to turn the hearts of the fathers to the children, and the disobedient to the wisdom of the just, to make ready a people prepared for the Lord."

## He was to be a prophet like Moses

O.T. Deuteronomy 18:17 "And the LORD said to me: 'What they have spoken is good. I will raise up for them a Prophet like you from among their brethren, and will put my words in His mouth, and He shall speak to them all that I command Him."

N.T. Acts 3:22-23 "Moses truly said to the fathers, 'The Lord your God will raise up for you a Prophet like me from your brethren. Him you shall hear in all things, whatever He says to you. And it shall be that every soul who will not hear that Prophet shall be utterly destroyed from among the people.'"

## He was to have an especial anointing of the Holy Spirit

O.T. Psalms 45:7 "Your throne, O God, is forever and ever; a scepter of righteousness is the scepter of your kingdom. You love righteousness and hate wickedness; Therefore God, Your God, has anointed you with the oil of gladness more than your companions."

O.T. Isaiah. 11:2 "The Spirit of the LORD shall rest upon Him, The Spirit of wisdom and understanding, The Spirit of counsel and might, The Spirit of knowledge and of the fear of the LORD."

N.T. Matthew 3:16 "When He had been baptized, Jesus came up immediately from the water; and behold, the heavens were opened to Him, and He saw the Spirit of God descending like a dove and alighting upon Him. And suddenly a voice came from heaven, saying, "This is my beloved Son, in whom I am well pleased".

## He was to be a priest after the order of Melchizedeck

O.T. Psalms 110:4 "The LORD has sworn and will not relent, 'You are a priest forever according to the order of Melchizedek.'"

N.T. Hebrews 5:5-6 "So also Christ did not glorify Himself to become High Priest, but it was He who said to Him: "You are My Son, Today I have begotten you". As He also says in another place: "You are a priest forever According to the order of Melchizedek."

## He would be sent to the Gentiles as well as the Jews

O.T. Isaiah 42:1-4 "Behold! My Servant whom I uphold, My Elect One in whom My Soul delights! I have put My Spirit upon Him; He will bring forth justice to the Gentiles. He will not cry out, nor raise His voice, nor cause His voice to be heard in the street. A bruised reed He will not break, and smoking flax He will not quench; He will bring forth justice for truth. He will not fail nor be discouraged, till He has established justice in the earth."

N.T. Matthew 12:18-21 "Behold, My servant, whom I have chosen; My beloved, in whom my soul is well pleased: I will put My Spirit upon him, and he shall show judgment to the Gentiles. He shall not strive, nor cry; neither shall any man hear his voice in the streets. A bruised reed shall he not break, and smoking flax shall he not quench, till he sends forth judgment unto victory. And in his name shall the Gentiles trust."

## His ministry was to begin in Galilee

O.T. Isaiah 9:1-2 "In Galilee of the Gentiles, the people who walked in darkness have seen a great light; those who dwelt in the land of the shadow of death, upon them a light has shined."

N.T. Matthew 4:12 2 "Now when Jesus had heard that John was cast into prison, he departed into Galilee; and leaving Nazareth, he came and dwelt in Capernaum, which is upon the sea coast, in the borders of Zebulon and Nephthalim: That it might be fulfilled which was spoken by Isaiah the prophet, saying, The land of Zebulon, and the land of Nephthalim, by the way of the sea, beyond Jordan, Galilee of the Gentiles; "The people which sat in darkness saw great light;

and to them which sat in the region and shadow of death, light is sprung up."

We have gone over enough scripture to prove that He fulfilled many, many prophecies. The following is a list that you can look up for yourself:

**Later He was to enter Jerusalem to bring salvation**

Zechariah 9:9

> Matthew 21:1-5

**He was to enter the temple**

Haggai 2:7-9

> Matthew 21:12

**His zeal for the Lord is spoken of in**

Psalms 69:9

> John 2:17

**His manner of teaching was to be by parables**

Psalms 78:2

> Matthew 13:34-35

**His ministry was to be characterized by miracles**

Isaiah 35:5-6

> Matthew 11:4-6

**He was to be rejected by his brethren, the Jews**

Psalms 69:8 & Isaiah 53:3

> John 1:11

**He would become a "stone of stumbling" and a "rock of offense" to the Jews**

Isaiah 8:14

> Romans 9:23

**He would be hated without a cause.**

Psalms 69:4 & Isaiah 49:7

John 7:48 & John 15:25

**He was to be rejected by the rulers**

Psalms 118:22

> Matthew 21:42 & John 7:48

**He would be betrayed by a friend**

Psalms 41:9, Psalms 55:12-14

> John 13:18, 21

**He was to be forsaken by his disciples**

Zechariah 13:7

> Matthew 26:31-56

**He was to be sold for 30 pieces of silver**

Zechariah 11:12

> Matthew 26:15

**His price (30 pieces of silver) was to be given to buy a potter's field**

Zechariah 11:13

> Matthew 27:7

**He was to be smitten on the cheek**

Micah 5:1

> Matthew 27:30

**He was to be spat on**

Isaiah 50:6

> Matthew 27:30

**He would be mocked**

Psalms 22:7-8

> Matthew 27:31, 39, & 44

**He would be beaten**

Psalms 50:6

> Matthew 26:67; 27:26, 30

**His death by crucifixion is given in detail in Psalm 22**

**The meaning of His death, as an atonement for our sins is given in Isaiah 53**

**His hands and feet were to be pierced**

Psalms 22:16

> John 19:18 & 37; 20:25

**Yet, not one of his bones were to be broken**

Exodus 12:46; Psalms 34:20

> John 19:33-36

**He was to suffer thirst**

Psalms 22:15

> John 19:28

**Be given vinegar to drink**

Psalms 69:21

> Matthew 27:34

**He was to be numbered with transgressors**

Isaiah 53:12

> Matthew 27:38

**However He was to be raised from the dead and His body was not to see corruption**

Psalms 16:10 Thou wilt not leave my soul in hell; neither wilt thou suffer thine Holy One to see corruption.

> Acts 2:31 He seeing this before spoke of the resurrection of Christ, that his soul was not left in hell, neither did his flesh see corruption.

**He was to ascend to the right hand of God**

Psalms 68:18 Thou hast ascended on high, Thou hast led captivity captive: Thou hast received gifts for men; yea, for the rebellious also, that the Lord God might dwell among them.

> Luke 24:51 It came to pass, while He blessed them, he was parted from them, and carried up into heaven.

Psalms 110:1 The Lord said unto my Lord, Sit Thou at my right hand, until I make Thine enemies Thy footstool.

Hebrews 1:3 Who being the brightness of His glory, and the express image of His person, and upholding all things by the word of His power, when He had by himself purged our sins, sat down on the right hand of the Majesty on high.

## CHRIST TESTIFIED TO THE FACT THAT HE FULFILLED OLD TESTAMENT PROPHECY

The Gospel of John was written to offer full proof, so that you might believe the Jesus of Nazareth is the Messiah that the Old Testament predicted would come, and this Messiah, this Jesus, is the Son of God. Moreover, you receive eternal life through believing on Him. John 5:39 "Search the Scriptures for they testify of me."

More than 40 false Messiahs have appeared in the history of the Jewish Nation, and not one of them ever appealed to fulfilled prophecy to establish their claims.

John 5:46 "If you had believed Moses, you would have believed me, for he wrote of me."

Matthew 5:17 "Jesus said, "I am not come to destroy the law and prophets . . . . but to fulfill them."

In the beginning of His ministry, he read to the People in the synagogue at Capernaum the most important Messianic Prophecy. Isaiah 61:1-2 "The Spirit of the Lord GOD is upon Me, Because the LORD has anointed Me To preach good tidings to the poor; He has sent Me to heal the brokenhearted, To proclaim liberty to the captives, and the opening of the prison to those who are bound; to proclaim the acceptable year of the LORD, and the day of vengeance of our God; To comfort all who mourn."

He quoted this prophecy in Luke 4:16-21, "He came to Nazareth, where he had been brought up and, as his custom was, he went into the synagogue on the Sabbath day, and stood up for to read. And there was delivered unto him the book of the prophet Isaiah. And when he had opened the book, he found the place where it was written, The Spirit of the Lord *is* upon me, because he hath anointed me to preach the gospel to the poor; he hath sent me to heal the brokenhearted, to preach deliverance to the captives, and recovering of sight to the blind, to set at liberty them that are bruised, To preach the acceptable year of the Lord. And he closed the book, and he gave it again to the minister, and sat down. And the eyes of all them that were in the synagogue were fastened on him. And he began to say unto them, this day is this scripture fulfilled in your ears." John 4:25-26 The woman said to Him, "I know that Messiah is coming" (who is called Christ). "When He comes, He will tell us all things." Jesus said to her, "I who speak to you am He."

When praising John the Baptist, Christ called attention to the fact that John was His forerunner, even as was predicted. So our Lord not only said that John came in fulfillment of prophecy, but that He, Jesus, was the One for whom John came to be the forerunner.

Luke 18:31 Then He took the twelve aside and said to them, "Behold, we are going up to Jerusalem, and all things that are written by the prophets concerning the Son of Man will be accomplished. He will be delivered to the Gentiles and will be mocked and insulted and spit upon. They will scourge Him and kill Him. And the third day He will rise again." Luke 24:27 "Beginning at Moses and all the Prophets, He expounded to them in all the Scriptures the things concerning Himself." Luke 24:44 "Then He said to them, "These are the words which I spoke to you while I was still with you, that all things must be fulfilled which were written in the Law of Moses and the Prophets and the Psalms concerning Me."

## THE DISCIPLES TELL US THAT JESUS IS THE MESSIAH

The backbone of Peter's sermon on the day of Pentecost was an argument from the Old Testament to prove to the Jews that Jesus of Nazareth whom they had crucified was the Messiah of which David had written:

Acts 22:22-26 "Men of Israel, hear these words: Jesus of Nazareth, a Man attested by God to you by miracles, wonders, and signs which God did through Him in your midst, as you yourselves also know—Him, being delivered by the determined purpose and foreknowledge of God, you have taken by lawless hands, have crucified, and put to death; Whom God hath raised up, having loosed the pains of death. David spoke concerning Him, I foresaw the Lord always before my face, for He is on my right hand, that I should not be moved: Therefore did my heart rejoice, and my tongue was glad; moreover also my flesh shall rest in hope."

Acts 13:29-30 When they had fulfilled all that was written of him, they took Him down from the tree, and laid Him in a sepulcher. But God raised Him from the dead.

## Paul testifies that Jesus is the Messiah

Acts 17:2-3 And Paul, as his manner was, went in unto them, and three Sabbath days reasoned with them out of the scriptures, explaining and demonstrating, that Christ must needs have suffered, and risen again from the dead; and that this Jesus, whom I preach unto you, is Christ.

1 Corinthians 15:1-4 Moreover, brethren, I declare unto you the gospel which I preached unto you, which also ye have received, and wherein ye stand; By which also ye are saved, if ye keep in memory what I preached unto you, unless ye have believed in vain. For I delivered unto you first of all that which I also received, how that Christ died for our sins according to the scriptures; And that He was buried, and that He rose again the third day according to the scriptures:

## GENEALOGIES PROVE JESUS IS THE MESSIAH

Usually, when we come to the "begats" in Matthew and Luke, we tend to skip over them because we can't remember all the people, but they are very important because only God could work out the Regal and Royal lineage of Jesus.

In 70 AD all the records (remember the census records when Jesus was born) were destroyed when Jerusalem was destroyed just as Jesus prophesied would happen.

**Matthew's genealogy** shows that Joseph is in the **regal** lineage of descent from King David, down through Solomon. But Joseph was also a descendant of David through Jeconiah, a certain evil man (Jeremiah 22:29-30 "Thus says the LORD: 'Write this man down as childless, a man who shall not prosper in his days; for none of his descendants shall prosper, sitting on the throne of David, And ruling anymore in Judah.") whose blood relatives God said would never sit on David's throne. Jesus had the regal lineage to the throne through Joseph but not a royal lineage. Matthew makes it perfectly clear that the seed of David, must be virgin-born, and yet have a legal right to the throne of David. Jesus was not from the bloodline of Joseph; the Holy Spirit was His father.

**Luke's genealogy** shows that Mary was in the **royal** lineage from King David, but she was not in the regal lineage, for she was a descendant of King David through Nathan, whereas the throne rights were to come to Jesus through Solomon's line.

In view of these Scriptures we see that Jesus had the Royal lineage through His Mother Mary and the regal lineage through His earthly father Joseph to rule as King.

### To summarize:

- Over 333 fulfilled prophecies prove Jesus Christ of the New Testament is the Jewish Messiah of the Old Testament.

- Christ testified to the fact that He fulfilled Old Testament prophecy.

- The disciples tell us that Jesus is the Messiah.

- The genealogies of Matthew & Luke prove that only Jesus is the Messiah.

# Chapter 6

## DO CHRISTIANS BELIEVE IN GHOSTS?

Since ghosts are usually associated with Halloween, witches, and warlocks, perhaps most Christians want to distance themselves from anything that appears to be from another realm. Whether one wants to admit it or not, most people know there is a spiritual realm that the natural man cannot perceive. Usually people whose lives have been lived in degradation on earth can attest to this fact. Many admit to encountering evil spirits or ghosts. Christians do not believe in ghosts in the sense that people's spirits return as ghosts. There is a supernatural realm where evil spirits abide. They are sometimes called seducing spirits. At times they can appear to be a dear departed relative to entice an unsuspecting victim into believing it is that loved one. However the Bible clearly teaches us there should not be one among Christians that conjures spells, or a medium, or a spiritualist, or one who calls up the dead, for all who do these things is an abomination to the Lord.[8] We do believe in the Holy Spirit or Holy Ghost and this is the one to which I want to introduce you.

In 1966, when I was approximately 32 years old there was no teaching about the Holy Ghost/Spirit in any of the churches I had attended. I was just like the Christians Paul was talking to in Acts when he said unto them, "Have ye received the Holy Ghost since ye believed?" My answer was the same as theirs, "We have not so much as heard whether there is any Holy Ghost."

We have come a long way since then, but for the most part we are still ignorant of the Holy Ghost. Many Bible translators have changed the word Ghost to Spirit in many instances in the Bible. Some think the Spirit was non-existent until the day of Pentecost. Others think of Him as a force. Some never think of Him at all. The Bible says He is One of the three that make up the triune God we serve.

They know God as Creator and Jesus as Savior, but they know nothing or little about the Holy Ghost/Spirit. From the Holy Bible they should be able to see that the Holy Spirit is a person, and He has a specific job to do.

## The Holy Spirit was in the Old Testament

Sometimes we think of the activity of the Holy Spirit as beginning on the day of Pentecost. But in fact the Old Testament is full of references to the Spirit of God.

While the term "Holy Spirit" is used only three times in the Old Testament, the related terms "Spirit" and "Spirit of God" are used in abundance. For example, Genesis 1:2 makes reference to the Spirit of God hovering over the surface of the deep as a participant in Creation. Also early on, the "wind" or breath", of God (meaning the Holy Spirit) is seen as a creative force and source of life. God breathed the "breath of life" into Adam in the Garden.[9] Much later, Ezekiel prophesied to the wind to blow over human bones, restoring life to them.[10]

Elsewhere, especially in the prophetic writings, the Spirit is seen as the source of supernatural power to speak and act. We read of the Spirit "coming upon" persons, enabling them to prophesy or perform some mighty deed. For instance, the "Spirit of God came upon" Saul so he could join the prophets at Gibeah in prophesying.[11]

Some of the most familiar passages we quote regarding the Holy Spirit from the Old Testament are:

Psalms 51:11 "Do not cast me from your presence or take your Holy Spirit from me."

Psalms 139:7 "Where can I go from your Spirit? Where can I flee from your presence?"

Isaiah 11:1, 2 "A shoot will come up from the stump of Jesse; from his roots a Branch will bear fruit. The Spirit of the Lord will rest on him—the Spirit of wisdom and of understanding, the Spirit of counsel and of power, the Spirit of knowledge and of the fear of the Lord."

Isaiah 61:1a "The Spirit of the Sovereign Lord is on me, because the Lord has anointed me to preach good news to the poor."

Zechariah 4:6b "Not by might nor by power, but by my Spirit, says the Lord Almighty."

Joel 2:28a "I will pour out my Spirit on all people."

This last reference summarizes a belief that there was coming a time when the Spirit's operation would change. No longer would His activity be restricted to a select few on isolated occasions. Rather, the Spirit would be available to all persons in fresh measure.

These are but a few of the references to the Spirit of God working thru lives in the Old Testament. However, the spirit was not given to every one of God's people.

## Evidence of the Holy Spirit in both testaments

Let's look at a few of the divine attributes of the Holy Spirit proving His deity as one of the three persons in the Godhead.

### He is eternal

Hebrews 9:13-14 "For if the blood of bulls and of goats, and the ashes of an heifer sprinkling the unclean, sanctified to the purifying of the flesh: How much more shall the blood of Christ, who through the eternal Spirit offered himself without spot to God, purge your conscience from dead works to serve the living God?"

### He is omnipresent (present everywhere)

Psalms 139:7-10 "Where can I go from Your Spirit? Or where can I flee from Your presence? If I ascend into heaven, You are there; if I make my bed in hell, behold, You are there, if I take the wings of the morning, and dwell in the uttermost parts of the sea, even there Your hand shall lead me; Your right hand shall hold me."

### He is omnipotent (all powerful)

Job 26:11 "The pillars of heaven tremble and are astonished at His reproof. He divided the sea with His power, and by his understanding He smites through the proud. By His spirit He hath garnished the heavens; His hand hath formed the crooked serpent. Lo, these are parts of His ways: but how little a portion is heard of Him? But the thunder of His power who can understand?"

### He is Omniscient (all knowing)

1 Corinthians 2:10-11 "But God hath revealed them unto us by His Spirit: for the Spirit searches all things, yea, and the deep things of God. For what man knows the things of a man, except the spirit of man, which is in him? Even so the things of God knows no man, but the Spirit of God."

## With what divine works is the Spirit associated?

### Creation

Genesis 1:2 "And the earth was without form, and void; and darkness was upon the face of the deep. And the Spirit of God moved upon the face of the waters."

### Regeneration

John 3:5-8 "Jesus answered, Verily, verily, I say unto thee, except a man be born of water and of the Spirit, he cannot enter into the kingdom of God. That, which is born, of the flesh is flesh; and that which is born of the Spirit is spirit."

### Sanctification

Romans 15:16 "I should be the minister of Jesus Christ to the Gentiles, ministering the gospel of God, that the offering up of the Gentiles might be acceptable, being sanctified by the <u>Holy Ghost.</u>"

### Resurrection

Romans 8:11 "But if the Spirit of Him that raised up Jesus from the dead dwells in you, He that raised up Christ from the dead shall also quicken your mortal bodies by His Spirit that dwells in you."

## Let us look briefly at some of the names given the Holy Ghost/ Spirit

Romans 15:16 "That I might be a minister of Jesus Christ to the Gentiles, ministering the gospel of God, that the offering of the Gentiles might be acceptable, sanctified by the Holy Spirit." He is called the <u>Holy Ghost.</u>

Luke 11:13 "If you then, being evil, know how to give good gifts to your children, how much more will your heavenly Father give the Holy Spirit to those who ask Him!"

Romans 8:9 "But you are not in the flesh but in the Spirit, if indeed the Spirit of God dwells in you. Now if anyone does not have the Spirit of Christ, he is not His."

John 14:15 "If you love me, keep my commandments. And I will pray the Father, and He will give you another Comforter (Helper), that He may abide with you forever—the Spirit of truth, whom the world cannot receive, because it neither sees Him nor knows Him; but you know Him, for He dwells with you and will be in you."

Ephesians 1:13 "In Him you also trusted, after you heard the word of truth, the gospel of your salvation; in whom also, having believed, you were sealed with the Holy Spirit of promise, who is the guarantee of our inheritance until the redemption of the purchased possession, to the praise of His glory."

Hebrews 10:29 "Of how much worse punishment, do you suppose, will he be thought worthy who has trampled the Son of God underfoot, counted the blood of the covenant by which he was sanctified a common thing, and insulted the Spirit of grace?"

Romans 8:2 "The law of the Spirit of life in Christ Jesus has made me free from the law of sin and death."

Romans 8:14-15 "As many as are led by the Spirit of God, they are the sons of God. For ye have not received the spirit of bondage again to fear; but ye have received the Spirit of adoption, whereby we cry, Abba, Father."

The names given in the preceding verses are: Holy Ghost, Holy Spirit, Spirit of God, Spirit of Christ, Comforter, Spirit of Truth, Holy Spirit of Promise, Guarantee, Spirit of Grace, Spirit of Life, and Spirit of Adoption.

## Representations or symbols which identify the Holy Spirit

### As the wind or breath

John 3:8 "The wind blows where it wishes and you hear the sound of it, but cannot tell where it comes from and where it goes. So is everyone who is born of the Spirit." The wind works mysteriously.

Genesis 2:7 "And the LORD God formed man of the dust of the ground, and breathed into his nostrils the breath of life; and man became a living soul." He is life giving.

Ezekiel 37:9-10 "Then said the Lord unto me, 'Prophesy unto the breath, prophesy, son of man, and say to the breath, 'Thus says the Lord GOD: "Come from the four winds, O breath, and breathe upon these slain, that they may live."'" "So I prophesied as he commanded me, and breath came into them, and they lived, and stood up upon their feet, an exceeding great army."

**Guarantee**

2 Corinthians 1:22 "He also has sealed us and given us the Spirit in our hearts as a guarantee."

Ephesians 1:13 "In Him you also trusted, after you heard the word of truth, the gospel of your salvation; in whom also, having believed, you were sealed with the Holy Spirit of promise, Who is the guarantee of our inheritance until the redemption of the purchased possession, to the praise of His glory." He is part of the purchase-money or property given in advance as security or guarantee for the rest.

2 Corinthians 5:5 "Now He who has prepared us for this very thing is God, who also has given us the Spirit as a guarantee."

**Seal**

Ephesians 1:13 "In Him you also trusted after you heard the word of truth, the gospel of your salvation; in whom also, having believed, you were sealed with the Holy Spirit of promise." The Holy Spirit is our seal.

2 Timothy 2:19 "Nevertheless, the solid foundation of God stands, having this seal: "The Lord knows those who are His." He is our confirmation or evidence of being redeemed.

**Fire**

Isaiah 4:4 "When the Lord has washed away the filth of the daughters of Zion, and purged the blood of Jerusalem from her midst, by the spirit of judgment and by the spirit of burning or (fire)." He sanctifies or makes holy.

Matthew 3:11-12 "I indeed baptize you with water unto repentance, but He who is coming after me is mightier than I, whose sandals I am not worthy to carry. He will baptize you with the Holy Spirit and fire." He consumes us like fire.

Jeremiah 20:9 Then I said, "I will not make mention of Him, nor speak anymore in His name. But His word was in my heart like a burning fire." He inspires us.

**Water**

John 7:37-39 "On the last day, that great day of the feast, Jesus stood and cried out, saying, "If anyone thirsts, let him come to Me and drink. He who believes in Me, as the Scripture has said, out of his heart will flow rivers of living water." But this He spoke concerning the Spirit, whom those believing in Him would receive; for the Holy Spirit was not yet given, because Jesus was not yet glorified." He satisfies the thirsty. The spirit will flow out of the heart like rivers of living water.

Ezekiel 47:8 "Then he said to me: "This water flows toward the eastern region, goes down into the valley, and enters the sea. When it reaches the sea, its waters are healed. And it shall be that every living thing that moves, wherever the rivers go, will live." Water is life giving; so is the Spirit of God.

**Dove**

Mark 1:10 "And immediately, coming up from the water, He saw the heavens parting and the Spirit descending upon Him like a dove. Then a voice came from heaven, "You are My beloved Son, in whom I am well pleased." In this passage there is a picture of the Holy Spirit as a dove hovering (suspending or floating) over Jesus.

**Oil**

Exodus 25:6 "To comfort all who mourn, to console those who mourn in Zion, to give them beauty for ashes, the oil of joy for mourning, the garment of praise for the spirit of heaviness."

Acts 10:38 "God anointed Jesus of Nazareth with the Holy Spirit and with power, who went about doing good and healing all who were oppressed by the devil, for God was with Him."

**Wine**

Ephesians 5:18-19 "Do not be drunk with wine, in which is dissipation; but be filled with the Spirit, speaking to one another in psalms and hymns and spiritual songs, singing and making melody in your heart to the Lord." He is the symbol of gladness.

Joel 1:10 "The field is wasted, the land mourns; for the grain is ruined, the new wine is dried up, the oil fails." He is the ingredient of worship.

Again from the Scriptures we can see Symbols that represent Him as: Wind or Breath, Guarantee, Seal, Fire, Water, Dove, Oil, and Wine.

## The Holy Spirit and Jesus Christ

In the gospels of Matthew, Mark, and Luke, the Holy Spirit is presented primarily as the enabler of Jesus' ministry. His public life began after His baptism, when the Spirit descended like a dove and remained upon Him.[12] Immediately after; Jesus was led by the Spirit into the wilderness, where He was tempted by Satan. Then Jesus returned to Galilee in the power of the Spirit.[13] For the rest of His earthly life, Jesus depended heavily upon the power of the Spirit within Him.

The Gospel of John adds another facet of understanding to our study of the Holy Spirit, for this book contains the bulk of Jesus' own teaching about the Spirit.

## The Holy Spirit and the Church

In the Book of Acts, the Holy Spirit is presented primarily as the source of power for Christians to witness and evangelize. Some have even suggested that the book could be more appropriately titled "The Acts of the Holy Spirit". On the day of Pentecost, a dramatic change came over the disciples, which Peter identified as the promise of Joel 2.[14] "This is that which was spoken by the prophet Joel; And it shall come to pass in the last days, says God, I will pour out of my Spirit upon all flesh: and your sons and your daughters shall prophesy, and your young men shall see visions, and your old men shall dream dreams: And on my servants and on my handmaidens I will pour out in those days of my Spirit; and they shall prophesy." The Holy Spirit was poured out on all the people gathered for worship.

In Paul's writings, one of the recurring themes is the contrast between life in the Spirit and life in the flesh. Paul made it clear that the filling of the Holy Spirit is not optional for believers. "If anyone does not have the Spirit of Christ, he does not belong to Christ."[15] In another letter, Paul said "Do not get drunk on wine, which leads to debauchery, instead, be filled with the Spirit."[16] Two distinct ministries of the Spirit may be identified in Paul's letters. Some have likened them to the images of wine and oil in Joel 2. Wine is taken into the body and makes changes on the inside. The Holy Spirit living in us is like wine. He convicts us of our sins and shortcomings and when we obey His prompting it produces the fruit of the Spirit;[17] changing us from the inside out. Oil, however, is for anointing the outside of the body. The gifts of the Holy Spirit,[18] which affect not our character but our ministries, are like oil. These gifts are used outside of the body for others. Paul spoke clearly about the relationship between these two ministries of the Spirit. The fruit must always accompany the gifts, which primarily is love.

So to answer the question, "Do Christians believe in Ghosts?" We believe in one Holy Ghost/Spirit. We do not conjure up ghosts or spirits of the dead. There shall not be found among you anyone who makes his son or his daughter pass through the fire, or one who practices witchcraft, or a soothsayer, or one who interprets omens, or a sorcerer, or one who conjures spells, a medium, a fortune teller, or one who calls up the dead. For all who do these things are an abomination to the Lord.[19]

Perhaps the most important message that can be spoken to today's church on the subject is that we need the Holy Spirit. It is possible to resist the Spirit, but it is much better to yield ourselves fully to Him. He is eager to transform our lives if we will but let Him.

# Chapter 7

## DOES THE DEVIL WEAR A RED SUIT
## AND CARRY A PITCHFORK?

N o, the devil or Satan doesn't wear a red suit and carry a pitchfork. Satan is good at disguising himself because we forget that he is alive and well on planet earth. As long as he can get people to ridicule him, or have them believe he is a figment of someone's imagination he is winning the battle in which most Christians don't have a clue they are fighting. Some people lightheartedly say "The devil made me do it." For the most part we go along our merry way, never realizing that he is our archenemy, who is at war with us on a daily basis. He is out to kill our faith, love, joy, peace, patience, kindness, and our ambition for good. He is out to steal and destroy our health, wealth, and relationships. Unless we know the truth about him, he will continue to rob us of all that is precious to us.

Hopefully you will learn who the devil is, his characteristics, where he originated and his purposes. I would like to share a few things I have learned about the devil, as we attempt to unmask him, to show who he really is.

A well-known evangelist in the eighties told an episode of a woman who came weeping to him with bitter tears. The story goes that her sixteen-year-old son had been given the family automobile for the first time. About midnight the police came knocking on her door. Her son had held up a convenience store operator so he could get money for drugs. When the operator resisted, her son shot and killed him and the son was in jail. The mother's questions were: "How could this happen in our family? We go to church. I have taught our son about Jesus. Why did God let it happen?" The evangelist's response was, "Did you ever teach him about the devil?" The mother said, "No, I never have." He then replied, "You mean you allowed your sixteen year old son to go out in the enemy's territory without knowing he had an enemy lurking about seeking whom he may devour?" "That would be the same as the United States Government sending its troops to a foreign country and not telling them they were at war with them, sending them off without any weapons and no knowledge of who the enemy was nor their tactics."

This is a true story. I wonder how many thousands of times something similar has been replayed. Parents have wondered, "How could this have happened to our son? We took him to church; we tried to teach him right from wrong. We did all we knew to do." The Lord says "My people are destroyed for a lack of knowledge."[20]

We must ask ourselves, "Where did Satan originate?" The Bible gives us the answer. "For by Him (God the Father) were all things created, that are in heaven, and that are in earth, visible and invisible, whether they be thrones, or dominions, or principalities, or powers: all things were <u>created</u> by Him and for Him."[21] This means Satan or Lucifer was created by God.

We know who he is not. The devil is not a cute little fellow running around in a little red suit with horns and a pitchfork.

So who is he? The moment of Satan's creation is not indicated in the Bible, but it was undoubtedly a long time ago. We do know his name was Lucifer; a bright, shining angel of light, and that he was perfect in his way, from the day that he was created. Most Bible scholars agree that the king of Tyre and Satan, or Lucifer is one and the same. Lucifer means light bearer.

In Ezekiel 28:11 we read:

Moreover the word of the LORD came to me, saying,
"Son of man, take up a lamentation for the king of Tyre,
and say to him, 'Thus says the Lord GOD:
"You were the seal of perfection,
full of wisdom and perfect in beauty.
You were in Eden, the garden of God;
Every precious stone was your covering:
The sardius, topaz, and diamond,
Beryl, onyx, and jasper,
Sapphire, turquoise, and emerald with gold.
The workmanship of your timbrels and pipes
(Apparently he was in charge of music.)

Was prepared for you on the day you were created.
You were the anointed cherub who covers;
I established you;
You were on the holy mountain of God;
You walked back and forth in the midst of fiery stones.
You were perfect in your ways from the day you were created,
Your heart was lifted up because of your beauty;
You were perfect in your ways from the day you were created,
till iniquity was found in you."

God gave this brilliant angel the power to exercise free will. He became proud of his beauty and ability. Instead of yielding to God's will, as was originally planned, he placed his will against God's will. As we can see he was very important when he was in the holy mountain of God, but then God cast him out. He was the most beautiful, perfect, and exalted being before iniquity was found in him. The next question is where did he go?

Let us look in Isaiah 14:12:

"How you are fallen from heaven,
O Lucifer, son of the morning!
How you are cut down to the ground,
You who weakened the nations!
For you have said in your heart:
"I will ascend into heaven,
I will exalt my throne above the stars of God;
I will also sit on the mount of the congregation
On the farthest sides of the north;
I will ascend above the heights of the clouds,
I will be like the Most High."
Yet you shall be brought down to Sheol,
To the lowest depths of the pit."

Satan, because of his diabolical ambition, became the object of prophecy. He is to be brought down to the lowest depths of the pit. This prophecy is yet to be fulfilled. However, the immediate result of his sin was a destructive fall and a change in his name from Lucifer to Satan. We learn so much about Satan just by his names.

## What are some of Satan's names that appear in the Scriptures

Isaiah 14:12-14—Here he is called **Lucifer**, son of the morning.

Matthew 10:25 He is called **Beelzebub** meaning Lord of Flies.

Isaiah 27:1—He is called **Leviathan or Dragon**.

Matthew 4:1-11—In the temptation of Jesus he is called the **tempter**, the **Devil** and **Satan**.

Matthew 9:34—But the Pharisees said, He casts out devils through the **prince of the devils**.

Matthew 13:19—He is called the **wicked one**. When anyone hears the word of the kingdom, and does not understand it, then the wicked one comes and snatches away what was sown in his heart.

Matthew 13:19 & 38—He answered and said to them: "He who sows the good seed is the Son of Man. The field is the world, the good seeds are the sons of the kingdom, but the tares are the sons of the **wicked one**. The **enemy** who sowed them is the **devil**, the harvest is the end of the age, and the reapers are the angels. Therefore as the tares are gathered and burned in the fire, so it will be at the end of this age.

John 12:31 Now is the judgment of this world: now shall the **prince of this world** be cast out. He is the prince, or ruler, of this world**.**

John 16:11 The **prince of this world** is judged.

2 Corinthians 4:4 "In whom the **god of this world** hath blinded the minds of them which believe not, lest the light of the glorious gospel of Christ, who is the image of God, should shine unto them."

2 Corinthians 11:14—"And no marvel; for Satan himself is transformed into an **angel of light**."

Ephesians 2:2—"Wherein in time past ye walked according to the course of this world, according to the **prince of the power of the air**, the spirit that now works in the children of disobedience."

1 Thessalonians 3:5—"For this reason, when I could no longer endure it, I sent to know your faith, lest by some means the **tempter** had tempted you, and our labor might be in vain."

Job 41:34—He beholds every high thing. He is king **over all the children of pride**.

## In the Bible we can see how diabolical Satan is by the things to which he is compared

Psalms 91:3 He is called a fowler (trapper). "Surely God shall deliver you from the snare of the **fowler** and from the perilous pestilence."

1 Peter 5:8 He is our adversary, he is as a roaring lion, he is the devourer. "Be sober; be vigilant; because your **adversary the devil** walks about like a **roaring lion**, seeking whom he may **devour**."

John 10:10 He is called the thief. "The **thief** cometh not, but for to steal and to kill, and to destroy."

John 10:12 He is called a wolf. "But a hireling, he who is not the shepherd, one who does not own the sheep, sees the **wolf** coming and leaves the sheep and flees; and the wolf catches the sheep and scatters them."

Revelation 12:9-10 He is called a dragon, that serpent of old, the Devil and Satan. "So the great **dragon** was cast out, that **serpent of old**, called the **Devil** and **Satan**, who deceives the whole world; he was cast to the earth, and his angels were cast out with him. Then I heard a loud voice saying in heaven, "Now salvation, and strength, and the kingdom of our God, and the power of His Christ have come, for the **accuser of our brethren**, who accused them before our God day and night, has been cast down." Here he is called the accuser of the brethren.

Revelation 20:2 He is called a dragon and serpent. "And he laid hold on the **dragon**, that **old serpent**, which is the **Devil**, and **Satan**."

Let's take a look at Satan's character. We have already seen he was the first rebel, the first sinner, and the first to gratify himself to wage war against all mankind.

John 8:44 He is the **father of lies**.

John 8:44 He is a **murderer**.

Matthew 13:39 He **sows discord**.

1 Peter 4:8 He is our **adversary**.

2 Corinthians 2:11 He is without principle taking advantage of men in their weak moments. "Be aware lest Satan should take advantage of us; for we are not ignorant of his devices."

## He is **cunning and deceitful.**

2 Corinthians 11:13-14 "Such are false apostles, deceitful workers, transforming themselves into apostles of Christ. And no wonder! For Satan transforms himself into an angel of light."

Revelation 12:10 "Then I heard a loud voice saying in heaven, "Now salvation, and strength, and the kingdom of our God, and the power of His Christ have come, for the accuser of our brethren, who accused them before our God day and night, has been cast down."

## He is **wicked.**

1 John 3:8 "He who sins is of the devil, for the devil has sinned from the beginning. For this purpose the Son of God was manifested, that He might destroy the works of the devil."

## He **slanders** God to man and man to God.

Job 1:8-12 "Then the LORD said to Satan, "Have you considered My servant Job, that there is none like him on the earth, a blameless and upright man, one who fears God and shuns evil?" So Satan answered the LORD and said, "Does Job fear God for nothing? Have You not made a hedge around him, around his household, and around all that he has on every side? You have blessed the work of his hands, and his possessions have increased in the land. But now, stretch out Your hand and touch all that he has, and he will surely curse You to Your face!" And the LORD said to Satan, "Behold, all that he has is in your power; only do not lay a hand on his person."

## He is **malignant**

Luke 8:12 "Those seed by the wayside are the ones who hear; then the devil comes and takes away the word out of their hearts, lest they should believe and be saved."

## He is **cowardly**

James 4:7 "Therefore submit to God. Resist the devil and he will flee from you"

He **blinds the mind**s of men.

2 Corinthians 2:2 "But even if our gospel is veiled, it is veiled to those who are perishing, whose minds the god of this age has blinded, who do not believe, lest the light of the gospel of the glory of Christ, who is the image of God, should shine on them."

Satan is **presumptuous**

Job 2:1-7 "Again there was a day when the sons of God came to present themselves before the LORD, and Satan came also among them to present himself before the LORD. And the LORD said to Satan, "From where do you come?" Satan answered the LORD and said, "From going to and fro on the earth, and from walking back and forth on it". Then the LORD said to Satan, "Have you considered My servant Job, that there is none like him on the earth, a blameless and upright man, one who fears God and shuns evil? And still he holds fast to his integrity, although you incited Me against him, to destroy him without cause." So Satan answered the LORD and said, "Skin for skin! Yes, all that a man has he will give for his life. But stretch out Your hand now, and touch his bone and his flesh, and he will surely curse You to Your face!" And the LORD said to Satan, "Behold, he *is* in your hand, but spare his life." So Satan went out from the presence of the LORD, and struck Job with painful boils from the sole of his foot to the crown of his head."

He is **prideful**

1 Timothy 3:6 "Let not a novice, lest being puffed up with pride he fall into the same condemnation as the devil."

He is **aggressive**

1 Peter 5:8 "Be sober, be vigilant; because your adversary the devil walks about like a roaring lion, seeking whom he may devour. Resist him, steadfast in the faith, knowing that the same sufferings are experienced by your brotherhood in the world."

He is **fierce and cruel**

Luke 9:38 "Suddenly a man from the multitude cried out, saying, "Teacher, I implore You, look on my son, for he is my only child. And behold, a spirit seizes him, and he suddenly cries out; it convulses him so that he foams at the mouth; and it departs from him with great difficulty."

Ephesians 6:10-18 "Finally, my brethren, be strong in the Lord and in the power of His might. Put on the whole armor of God that you may be able to stand against the wiles of the devil. We do not wrestle against flesh and blood, but against principalities, against powers, against the rulers of the darkness of this age, against spiritual hosts of wickedness in the heavenly places."

## Let us think of some of the methods and purposes of Satan as he fights against the children of God.

He keeps men in subjection and keeps them from turning to God. If he fails in this, he tries to kill the believer's testimony and ruin his influence for God.

If one falls he tries to make him stay fallen or commit suicide. He endeavors to cause men to end their lives by insisting it is the best way out; but he hides the true fact that this will be only the beginning of real torment in eternal hell.

He tries to get others in a lukewarm condition and if he succeeds, urges them to stay in that condition so that God will cut them off in the end.

He dares men to do many things, which they would not do under ordinary circumstances, and men are foolish enough to think they are not brave if they do not accept his dares.

Makes people think they are missing out on life if they do not go into all kinds of sin that in the end will damn their souls.

He emphasizes sin and sinful pleasures as innocent enjoyment.

Stirs unholy passions in men and women causing them to throw away all restraint and live a life of revelry.

Tries to make people think there is no joy in serving the Lord. This is one of his greatest errors. Serving Christ and winning souls who will be forever thankful, pays the greatest dividends, and affords the greatest pleasures known.

He convinces the diligent in business that he must spend all his time getting rich before serving the Lord. While the fact is that if one will truly serve the Lord he can be abundantly successful with God's help.

Urges churches and their leaders to make religion a paying proposition by appealing to the rich and influential through lowering the standards of holy living, making salvation easy for all, compromising essentials of the faith, feeding the sheep messages on current events and book reviews instead of the Word of God.

Last but not least, when he succeeds in tempting you—He will take you farther than you wanted to go, cost you more than you wanted to pay, and he will keep you longer than you wanted to stay!

## So what have we learned about the Devil, Lucifer or Satan?

He was created by God. He lived in heaven with God; he was a very beautiful angel with authority. He had a free will just as man has a free will. He was the Son of the Morning and the Angel of Light. He became proud because of his beauty and authority. He exercised his free will. He could do as he chose, so he chose to become like Almighty God. For this he and a third of the angels were cast down to the ground. He is now the god of this world, the prince of devils and ruler of this world, and the king over all the children of pride and of the power of the air.

We know that he is the father of all lies, that he can appear to be what he is not, that he is a deceiver, a murderer and he has come to kill, steal and destroy. He is our enemy, our adversary, the tempter, he is wicked and he sows discord. He is known as the lord of the flies or (dung heap) a dragon, a thief, and a wolf. He is malignant, cowardly, prideful, aggressive, fierce and cruel, cunning and sly. He lays a trap for unsuspecting people. He is without principle and takes advantage of us in our weak moments. He slanders God to man and man to God. He wants to keep us blinded to who he is and what he is doing.

He is the enemy of Jesus Christ. He put it in Herod's heart to kill all the new born babies under two years old when he heard Jesus was born trying to destroy him. He hates Jesus and he doesn't want people to choose Jesus over him. He wants to take as many to Hell with him as he can.

Satan is a defeated foe, and he has absolutely no authority over the believer except what we allow. We have a diabolical enemy who speaks to us in our mind; one whom we cannot see. As long as we are ignorant of his devices, he usually wins; and we don't even realize we are at war!

It is my prayer that you leave today a little less ignorant of him and his devices, and more prepared to do battle with the enemy. No longer will you think he is a cute little guy dressed up just to make us laugh.

*"Satan's greatest lie is to try to get us to think he does not exist."*
—C.S. Lewis

# Chapter 8

## IS IT SIN OR IS IT SICKNESS?

So many of our bad choices defy God's laws, and the consequences we incur are labeled sickness or disease. A good example of ascribing good to evil is the following prayer by Dr. Billy Graham.

"Heavenly Father, we come before you today to ask your forgiveness and to seek your direction and guidance. We know Your Word says, 'Woe to those who call evil good,' but that is exactly what we have done. We have lost our spiritual equilibrium and reversed our values. We have exploited the poor and called it the lottery. We have rewarded laziness and called it welfare. We have killed our unborn and called it choice. We have shot abortionists and called it justifiable. We have neglected to discipline our children and called it building self esteem. We have abused power and called it politics. We have coveted our neighbor's possessions and called it ambition. We have polluted the air with profanity and pornography and called it freedom of expression. We have ridiculed the time-honored values of our forefathers and called it enlightenment. Search us, Oh God, and know our hearts today; cleanse us from sin and Set us free. Amen!"

Most of us can't see that we have sinned. We rationalize, or better yet the devil speaks to us and says in first person singular: "I don't smoke, drink, or chew and don't go with those that do! "Well, I'm better than so & so and they claim to be a Christian so I am okay." "Everyone else is doing it and if it's all right for them, it's all right for me!" "It's not sin; it's a sickness." "My associates are hosting this party, they are doing it, and I have to fit in if I am to keep my job." "Don't be so narrow—minded; they will think you are a prude!" Sound familiar? Guess who is talking to you?

The word Sin in the New Testament is derived from the Greek word (ham-ar-tan'-o) which means to miss the mark; so as not to share in the prize.

Webster's dictionary says sin is an offense against God; a transgression against the law of God; misdeed, or fault; a perverted state of human nature in which the self is estranged from God.

Neil Anderson's definition of sin is living your life independent of God.

What a profound statement. Don't most of us do just that? Living our lives doing what we want to do, going where we want to go, without consciously asking God what He wants.

The Bible has a lot to say about sin. Therefore to him that knows to do good and doeth it not, to him it is sin.[22] Whosoever commits sin transgresses also the law: for sin is the transgression of the law.[23] We have to ask ourselves, "What is the law?" We certainly know the law is given in the Ten Commandments in the Old Testament.

- **Thou shall have no other Gods before Me.**

- **You shall not make unto yourselves any graven image, or any likeness of anything that is in heaven above or that is in the earth beneath or in the water under the earth.**

- **Thou shall not take the name of the Lord in vain.**

- **Remember the Sabbath to keep it holy.**

- **Honor your Father and Mother.**

- **You shall not kill.**

- **You shall not commit adultery.**

- **You shall not steal.**

- **You shall not bear false witness.**

- **You shall not covet.**[24]

Jesus sums up all the law for us in the New Testament. The Pharisees asked Jesus, "Teacher, which is the great commandment in the law?" Jesus said to him, "You shall love the Lord your God with all your heart, with all your soul, and with all your mind. This is the first and great commandment. And the second is like it: 'You shall love your neighbor as yourself.' On these two commandments hang all the Law and the Prophets."[25]

Most need no explanation, for example: For whatsoever is not of faith is sin [26]and all unrighteousness is sin.[27] Since the unrighteous did not like to retain God in their knowledge, God gave them over to a debased mind, to do those things which are not fitting; being filled with all unrighteousness, sexual immorality, wickedness, covetousness, maliciousness; full of envy, murder, strife, deceit, evil-mindedness; they are whisperers, backbiters, haters of God, violent, proud, boasters, inventors of evil things, disobedient to parents, undiscerning, untrustworthy, unloving, unforgiving, unmerciful; who, knowing the righteous judgment of God, that those who practice such things are deserving of death, not only do the same but also approve of those who practice them.[28]

A reprobate mind does all unrighteousness (vices against justice and every thing that keeps us in right standing with God), fornication (unlawful sexual sins), wickedness, covetousness, and maliciousness. It is full of envy, murder, debate (strife), deceit, malignity. It causes discord & strife; whisperers, backbiting, haters of God. They are despiteful, proud, boasters, inventors of evil things, disobedient to parents, without understanding, covenant breakers, without natural affection, implacable. You can't placate or please them; they are unmerciful and rebellious.

There is within man an innate knowledge of sin. A person knows when he is doing something he shouldn't do. His conscience tells him it is the wrong thing to do. The longer he persists in practicing sin, the more his conscience becomes dull of hearing that inner voice. They that are in the flesh cannot please God.[29]

The works of the flesh are: Adultery, fornication, uncleanness, lasciviousness, idolatry, witchcraft, hatred, variance, emulations, wrath, strife, seditions, heresies, envying, murders, drunkenness, and revelry.

It has been said the seven deadly sins are: pride, envy, gluttony, lust, anger, greed, and sloth.

## There are two kinds of sins

A presumptuous sin is one committed willfully, knowingly, and openly in defiance of the law.

A sin of ignorance is an act of breaking the law without knowing that the law is being violated.

## Where did sin originate

Ezekiel 28:15 gives us an account of the first sin which occurred in heaven when Lucifer rebelled against God. God gave this brilliant angel the power to exercise free will. He became proud of his beauty and ability. Instead of yielding to God's will, as was originally planned, he placed his will against God's will. The immediate result of his sin was a destructive fall and a change in his name from Lucifer to Satan. We have already seen he was the first rebel, the first sinner and the first to consecrate his self to wage war against all society.

## First sin on the earth

Genesis gives us the account of man's first sin in the Garden of Eden. And the Lord God commanded the man saying, "Of every tree of the garden you may freely eat; but of the tree of the knowledge of good and evil you shall not eat, for in the day that you eat of it you shall surely die."30 Adam was innocent and he had only one commandment to keep. Now we have many but Adam only had one!

We read in Genesis 3:1-6 The serpent was more cunning than any beast of the field which the Lord God had made. And he said to the woman, "Has God indeed said, 'You shall not eat of every tree of the garden'?" And the woman said to the serpent, "We may eat the fruit of the trees of the garden; but of the fruit of the tree which is in the midst of the garden, God has said, 'You shall not eat it, nor shall you touch it, lest you die.'" Then the serpent said to the woman, "You will not surely die. For God knows that in the day you eat of it your eyes will be opened and you will be like God, knowing good and evil." So when the woman saw that the tree was good for food, that it was pleasant to the eyes, and a tree desirable to make one wise, she took of its fruit and ate. She also gave to her husband with her, and he ate. Then the eyes of both of them were opened, and they knew that they were naked; and they sewed fig leaves together and made themselves coverings.

This shows man's failure to obey, the temptation of the devil, and Adam's fall from fellowshipping with God face to face.

The immediate effect was death came on mankind. Death actually means separation. Adam did not die a physical death when he was banished from the Garden of Eden because Scripture tells us he lived to be nine hundred and thirty years old. However, he became separated from the presence of God.

## What happened when sin entered the Garden of Eden?

- By one man's disobedience sin entered the world, and because of this we are all born with a sin nature. This means we have a tendency to live our lives independent of God.

- Adam and Eve were separated from God's presence.

They were cast out of the Garden of Eden. Prior to this event, every need they had been met, they lived in peace and harmony, they were in fellowship with God on a continual basis, and they lived in a state of bliss! Can you imagine the fear that came upon them when they were banished from the Garden of Eden into the harsh world of reality? This was probably the most awesome event in human history. Think about it. They went from having every need met to having to supply everything themselves.

To the woman He said: "I will greatly multiply your sorrow and your conception; in pain you shall bring forth children; your desire shall be for your husband, And he shall rule over you." Then to Adam He said, "Because you have heeded the voice of your wife, and have eaten from the tree of which I commanded you, saying, 'You shall not eat of it': "Cursed is the ground for your sake; in toil you shall eat of it All the days of your life. Both thorns and thistles it shall bring forth for you, and you shall eat the herb of the field. In the sweat of your face you shall eat bread till you return to the ground, for out of it you were taken; for dust you are, and to dust you shall return."[31]

- Adam lost dominion over the earth when he chose to obey Satan. He became his servant. Do you not know that to whom you yield yourselves servants to obey, his servants you are to whom you obey.[32]

- The devil became the Father of the unsaved. You are of your father the devil, and the desires of your father you want to do. He was a murderer from the beginning, and does not stand in the truth, because there is no truth in him. When he speaks a lie, he speaks from his own resources, for he is a liar and the father of it.[33]

- Hell is the destination of the unsaved.

## Who tempts us to sin?

The devil is the one who is known as the tempter. Then Jesus was led up by the Spirit into the wilderness to be tempted by the devil. And when He had fasted forty days and forty nights, afterward He was hungry. Now when the tempter came to Him, he said, "If You are the Son of God, command that these stones become bread."[34]

## How are we tempted to sin?

The devil speaks to us in our minds. He gives us vain imaginations and causes us to have evil thoughts.

The book of James tells us every man is tempted when he is drawn away of his own lust and enticed.

## What are the lusts that tempt mankind?

1 John 2:16 All that is in the world, the **lust of the flesh**, the **lust of the eyes**, and **the pride of life** is not of the Father, but of the world (ruled by Satan).

- Jesus was tempted by the same three things with which we are tempted.
- He was hungry—the lust of the flesh.
- He saw with his eyes all that could be his—the lust of the eye.
- He could have all power and glory now—the pride of life.

## The effects of Sins

The curse of Adam and Eve was put on mankind and we are still under that curse. We are born with a sin nature and are under the influence of Satan. Let's look at Adam and Eve. They ate from the tree of the knowledge of good and evil. From that point on they no longer lived by faith in God. Their judgment on how to live was now based on their five senses: what they could hear, see, taste, touch, and smell. Adam became a victim of the intellectual world when they ate of the tree of the knowledge of good and evil; with his faith being transferred from God, to faith into what he thought was best for himself. They no longer had an intimate relationship with God.

Because of Adam's disobedience, we are all born with a sinful nature. In our unregenerate state (before we are born again), we do not have a relationship with God. We know something **about** God, but we don't **know** God. Adam suffered no negative emotions until he sinned.

After Adam sinned:

Acceptance was replaced by rejection; therefore, we have a need to belong.

Innocence was replaced by guilt and shame; therefore, we have a need for our self-worth to be restored.

Faith was replaced by fear; therefore, we are afraid of dying.

Guilt, anger, and depression came because of sin.

Their authority was replaced by weakness and helplessness; therefore we have a need for strength and self-control.

Therefore, just as through one man sin entered the world, and death through sin, and thus death spread to all men, because all sinned. Therefore, as through one man's offense judgment came to all men, resulting in condemnation, even so through one Man's righteous act the free gift came to all men, resulting in justification of life. By one man's (Adam) sin death reigns and all were made sinners.[35]

As it is written: "There is none righteous, no, not one; There is none who understands; There is none who seeks after God. There is none who does good, no, not one." They have all turned aside; They have together become unprofitable."[36]

So according to the above, everyone is sinful and guilty before God, for all have sinned and fallen short of the glory of God.

According to what we have just read we have all sinned and in Ezekiel it says the soul that sins it shall die.[37] We all know that eventually we will die a natural death but this is talking about eternal separation from God.

Your iniquities have separated you and your God, and your sins have hid his face from you, that he will not hear.[38] Until a person asks God to forgive him for sinning and accepts Jesus Christ as the perfect sacrifice to cleanse him from sin he is still separated from God.

## Paul discusses our responsibility for sin

**Romans 2:1-8** "Therefore you are inexcusable, O man, whoever you are who judge, for in whatever you judge another you condemn yourself; for you who judge practice the same things. But we know that the judgment of God is according to truth against those who practice such things. And do you think this, O man, you who judge those practicing such things, and doing the same, that you will escape the judgment of God? Or do you despise the riches of His goodness, forbearance, and longsuffering, not knowing that the goodness of God leads you to repentance? But in accordance with your hardness and your impenitent heart you are treasuring up for yourself wrath in the day of wrath and revelation of the righteous judgment of God, who "will render to each one according to his deeds". Eternal life to those who by patient continuance in doing good seek for glory, honor, and immortality; but to those who are self-seeking and do not obey the truth, but obey unrighteousness— indignation and wrath, tribulation and anguish, on every soul of man who does evil, of the Jew first and also of the Greek; but glory, honor, and peace to everyone who works what is good, to the Jew first and also to the Greek." There is no partiality with God.

## Degrees in Sin

**Luke 7:41** "There was a certain creditor who had two debtors. One owed five hundred denarii's, and the other fifty. And when they had nothing with which to repay, he freely forgave them both. Tell Me, therefore, which of them will love him more?" Simon answered and said, "I suppose the one whom he forgave more." And He said to him, "You have rightly judged." Then He turned to the woman and said to Simon, "Do you see this woman? I entered your house; you gave Me no water for My feet, but she has washed My feet with her tears and wiped them with the hair of her head. You gave Me no kiss, but this woman has not ceased to kiss My feet since the time I came in. You did not anoint My head with oil, but this woman has anointed My feet with fragrant oil. Therefore I say to you, her sins, which are many, are forgiven, for she loved much. But to whom little is forgiven, the same loves little." Then He said to her, "Your sins are forgiven."

## The Progressiveness of Sin

**1 Kings 16:30** "Now Ahab the son of Omri did evil in the sight of the LORD, more than all who were before him. And it came to pass, as though it had been a trivial thing for him to walk in the sins of Jeroboam the son of Nebat that he took as wife Jezebel the daughter of Ethbaal, king of the Sidonians; and he went and served Baal and worshipped him. Then he set up an altar for Baal in the temple of Baal, which he had built in Samaria. And Ahab made a wooden image. Ahab did more to provoke the LORD God of Israel to anger than all the kings of Israel who were before him."

## Sins progressiveness exemplified in Joseph's brethren

First Jealousy

Genesis 37:4 But when his brothers saw that their father loved him more than all his brothers, they hated him and could not speak peaceably to him.

Then Conspiracy

Genesis 37:18 Now when they saw him afar off, even before he came near them, they conspired against him to kill him.

Finally, Murder

Genesis 37:20 Come therefore, let us now kill him and cast him into some pit;

## How are sins overcome?

In the Old Testament an animal sacrifice was required to have people's sins rolled back for a year. In the New Testament Jesus Christ was sacrificed to have our sins washed away completely and forever.

John 1:29 "The next day John saw Jesus coming to him and said, "Behold the Lamb of God which takes away the sin of the world.""

When we understand that we are sinners in need of a savior to keep us from going to hell, we ask the same question as the people asked on the day of Pentecost.

Acts 2:38 "What shall we do to be saved? Peter said "Repent and be baptized every one of you in the name of Jesus Christ for the remission of sins, and you shall receive the gift of the Holy Spirit."

Isaiah 1:18 "Come now, and let us reason together, says the Lord: though your sins be as scarlet, they shall be as white as snow; though they be red like crimson, they shall be as wool."

Psalms 103:12 "As far as the east is from the west, so far hath he removed our transgressions from us! How far is that?"

Because of our old sin nature we have to choose daily not to act like our old man acted. Satan is still out there to tempt us, and we have to resist him. Sometimes we err and sin against God, but he has made a way for us to repent and be forgiven.

How can this be? Is this merely a theological truth we are to accept? Should it have a practical outworking in our life? How does Christ truly deliver us?

The answer is so simple we often do not get it. It is too simple for the Hindus, who reject it in favor of works. They would rather crawl for miles to try to pacify God over their sins. Jews also reject this truth; they try to keep six hundred and thirty-three laws. Muslims would rather prostrate themselves and perform deeds, trying to appease Allah for their shortcomings. Even many Christians would rather add some rule of self reliance to their deliverance. They make promises to God and try to beat down all the desires of their flesh in their own strength. Here is the simple, uncomplicated gospel: whenever there is genuine repentance, there is instant forgiveness. There is instant cleansing, as well as continual openness to the throne of God. If we believe these truths, we are made free.

1 John 1:9 "If we confess our sins, he is faithful and just to forgive us our sins, and to cleanse us from all unrighteousness."

Romans 10:26 "If we sin willfully after we have received the knowledge of the truth, there remains no more sacrifice for sins"

Romans 7:23 "O wretched man that I am! Who shall deliver me from the body of this death? Paul answers his own question in the next verse: I thank God—through Jesus Christ our Lord! In other words, Jesus Christ set me free from the power and dominion of sin. So then, with the mind I serve the law of God, but with the flesh the law of sin."

2 Corinthians 10:5 "Cast down imaginations, and every high thing that exalts itself against the knowledge of God, and bringing into captivity every thought to the obedience of Christ." We must be very careful what we think. If we find ourselves thinking wrong thoughts we must bring our thinking back to the Word of God.

We have discussed the origin of sin. We have talked about the insidious ways sin creeps into our lives. We have seen that in most cases we willingly make wrong choices that bring consequences of those decisions. Many times those consequences cause us to have dis-ease and it can be treated, i.e. drunkenness and addictions. Many times just confessing our rebellion and disobedience to God and asking for His forgiveness cleanses us from all unrighteousness. After asking God to forgive us and cleanse us, we are at peace with Him and we feel no "dis-ease".

# Chapter 9

## WHO AM I?

A ll of us know that our body is not the real me. It's just made up of flesh, hair, features, tissue, and our internal organs. Quite a magnificent thing, but that's not me. It is just a housing for the real me. For many years I did not know that man is a triune being (three-in-one). I did not know there was a difference between my soul and my spirit; I thought they were one and the same.

To answer the question "Who Am I?" we are going to first establish the fact that there are three parts that constitute man. In 1 Thessalonians 5:23 we read, "Now may the God of Peace Himself sanctify you completely; and may your whole spirit, soul, and body be preserved blameless at the coming of the Lord Jesus Christ." From this we know three parts make up our being.

- With our bodies (the house in which we live) we contact the physical realm.

  The body is not the real you! It is just an earth suit. Your earth suit is left behind when you die.

- With our soul (man's intellect, emotions, will) we contact the mental or intellectual realm.

  The soul is not the real you! The mind, emotions, and will may not function, but a person can still live. You can lose all five senses and still be alive.

- With our spirit (the part of man that knows God) we contact the spiritual realm or our heavenly Father.

  Your spirit is the real you! The body without the spirit is dead.[39]

Hebrews 4:12 "The Word of God is living and powerful and sharper than any two-edged sword piercing even to the division of soul and spirit." This says the soul and the spirit are two different things! It also says God's Word plays a very important role in separating the soul and the spirit. Psychologists tell us that our soul is made up of our minds, our emotions, and our will. We need to see ourselves as a spiritual being rather than a physical being. We spend our time and money improving our body, educating our mind or soul, but ignoring the spirit or that part of man that lives forever. I like to think of it as man is a **spirit**, and he has a **soul** and lives in a **body**.

Theologians tell us that our spirit is made up of our conscience, discernment, and capacity for worship. The soul and the spirit make up the inner man or the heart of man. We know out of the abundance of the heart the mouth speaks.[40] Therefore, guard your heart with all diligence for out of it are the issues of life.[41]

First we will look at the natural man, the man of flesh, the carnal man, or the soul of man. Some call it man's unregenerate state (not restored to original strength or properties); some call it the depravity of man (marked by corruption or evil), which simply means man has not been regenerated or as Christians call it, "Born Again."

Let's take a look at the origin of man according to the Bible. God said, before I formed you in the womb I knew you.[42] "That which is born of flesh is flesh; and that which is born of the Spirit is spirit".[43] We know that when we are born of our earthly parents, we are the natural man, the man of flesh; we are carnal and we have a soulish nature.

What is man that you are mindful of him? And the son of man, that You visit him? For You have made him a little lower than the angels, and You have crowned him with glory and honor. You have made him to have dominion over the works of Your hands; You have put all things under his feet, all sheep and oxen—even the beasts of the field, the birds of the air and the fish of the sea that pass through the paths of the sea.[44] God said, "Let Us make man in Our image, according to Our likeness; let him have dominion over the fish of the sea, over the birds of the air, and over the cattle, over all the earth and over every creeping thing that creeps on the earth." So God created man in His own image; in the image of God He created him; male and female He created them. Then God blessed them, and God said to them, "Be fruitful and multiply; fill the earth and subdue it".[45] And the Lord God formed man of the dust of the ground, and breathed into his nostrils the breath of life; and man became a living being.[46] The Lord God planted a garden eastward in Eden; and there he put the man whom he had formed to dress it and to keep it.

We know that Adam, the first man and Eve the first woman were created in the likeness of God. Man was created a little lower than the angels and was given dominion over every living thing on the earth. Man was made from the dust of the earth. God breathed into man's nostrils and man became a living being.

As we consider this first man God created, we discover: After Adam was formed of the dust of the earth he became physically alive! His body was in union with his soul and spirit. In this life you cannot exist without your physical body or your earth suit. With our physical body we contact the physical realm. Adam was spiritually alive! God is a Spirit and only a spirit can contact a spirit.

Adam was given a significant, divine purpose for being here: to tend the garden and rule over all God's creatures. Adam had to use his mental abilities or his intellect to fulfill his purpose. Adam enjoyed a sense of safety and security. He had all his needs provided. Adam and Eve experienced a sense of belonging in that perfect garden. They evidently enjoyed an intimate, one-on-one, face-to-face communion with God.

Adam had it made in the Garden of Eden! He lived in the most wonderful place on earth. Talk about harmony, peace, bliss, and living in Paradise. No work, no weeds, no pestilence, Adam was in charge of dressing and keeping the garden. He knew God his Father on an intimate basis, had absolute faith in God, and there was only one wrong choice he could make. What was that? "Of every tree of the garden you may freely eat; but of the tree of the knowledge of good and evil you shall not eat, for in the day that you eat of it you shall surely die."[47]

We know the serpent tempted Eve, and she ate of the tree, she gave some to Adam, and he ate also. Did Adam die physically? No. In the natural Adam lived to be 930 years old; however the process of death was set in motion. Death really means separation. They died spiritually because of their disobedience. Their sin separated them from God, just as sin separates us from God to this day. Their union with God was destroyed. Because of this one act, mankind is born into this world separated from God. Mankind is spiritually dead because of Adam's trespass and sin. Adam and Eve lost their innocence; they fell from the wonderful state they enjoyed.

We hear so many people talk about the fall of man. What do they mean? He fell from the position he had with God. He had walked and talked with God face to face. Now there is an invisible wall that the natural man cannot pass. The Bible says God does not hear sinners except when they call on Him to save them.

By a single act of rebellion against God, Adam and Eve had declared their independence. They overtly challenged the right of Almighty God to guide and direct their lives, deciding to exercise their own will and power over themselves. The big "**I**", self, or ego began to rule and reign in men's lives; therefore, by one man, Adam, sin entered into the world and death by sin; and so death passed upon all men, for all have sinned. "For as by one man's disobedience many were made sinners."[48]

Because of Adam's sin, mankind has been affected forever since the fall. By one man's disobedience, sin entered the world; now we are all born with a sin nature. It is innate in man to live our lives independent of God. Adam and Eve were banished from God's presence. They were cast out of the Garden of Eden, and because of their act of disobedience our natural man does not have access to God the Father. The curse of Adam and Eve was put on mankind. We lost dominion over the earth when Adam chose to obey Satan. We are born into the world under Satan's dominion. We find ourselves in bondage to sin. Do you not know that to whom you yield yourselves servants to obey, his servants you are to whom you obey.[49] The devil became the Father of the unsaved[50]. Hell is now the destination of the unsaved.

To everyone's detriment, Adam and Eve no longer lived by faith in God. They had eaten from the knowledge of the tree of good and evil, and their judgment on how to live was now based on their five senses. What they could hear, see, taste, touch, and smell was what governed them. Adam became a victim of his own judgment.

They no longer had an intimate relationship with God. In the natural or unregenerate state, men know something about God, but they don't know God because they have no relationship with Him. Great fear replaced faith; now Adam and Eve were left to their own devices. Most of all they lost their peace because they had no fellowship with God. Anger and depression came because of sin. Acceptance was replaced by rejection; therefore, man has a need to belong. Innocence was replaced by guilt and shame; therefore, man has a need for his self-worth to be restored. His authority was replaced by weakness and helplessness; therefore, he has a need for strength and control.

When we are born into the world, we are born a natural man with a sin nature, separated from God, fearful, having a poor self-image, weak, and helpless. We are children of darkness, the devil is our father, and hell is our destination.

## What does the Bible say about our flesh, the natural man, the carnal man, and our old man?

From our mother's womb we are born of the flesh. That which is born of the flesh is flesh, and that which is born of the Spirit is spirit.[51] Those who are in the flesh cannot please God.[52] Speaking of when the body dies "It is sown a natural body, it is raised a spiritual body. There is a natural body and there is a spiritual body.[53] To be carnally minded is death, but to be spiritually minded is life and peace. Because the carnal mind is at war against God; for it is not subject to the law of God, nor indeed can be.[54] Before a person is born again he is carnal or living in the flesh. Before he is born again he is called the natural man. The natural man does not receive the things of the Spirit of God, for they are foolishness to him; nor can he know them, because they are spiritually discerned.[55] The law is spiritual, but I am carnal (our human nature), sold under sin. Before a person is born again he is carnal or living in the flesh. After he is born again he is told to put off concerning his former conduct, the old man which grows corrupt according to the deceitful lusts.[56]

Now that we have established that we are made up of body, soul, and spirit, and that the natural or soul man is our flesh, we need to consider the components of our natural man.

The first component is our mind. Our mind is like a computer. The data stored in our brain has come through what we have been taught by our parents, teachers, peers, television, books, the experiences of life, etc. Our actions originate from what has been fed into our computer; therefore, an unsaved person's conscience or thought process is not going to be the same as a Christian's.

The second component is our emotions or feelings. Our emotions feed into our computer. If they are negative they cause us to react in a negative way. If they are positive we react in a positive way. Without adhering to Christian Principles our emotions can rule our lives. If we don't bring our emotions in line with the Word of God, we can go to our graves allowing anger, hate, envy, jealousy, bitterness, self-pity, and un-forgiveness, etc. to destroy our lives.

Thirdly we are made up of our will. Our will compels us to do what we do, as dictated by our mind and our emotions. The first thing a child learns is to exercise his will. **I** will be fed, **I** will be changed, **I** will have **my** way, or **I** will scream. Foolishness is bound in the heart of every child but the rod of correction runs it from him.[57] Our will looks out for the Big "**I**." Unregenerate man is characterized by selfishness. Can you name one crime ever committed that the underlying cause was not selfishness?

Because of Adam's fall and everything we lost, we are all born with an emptiness or "hole" in our "heart". Some preachers call it a God hole that only God can fill, but man tries. We spend millions developing and exercising our bodies and our minds. We try to fill the hole in our hearts with the lust of the flesh or our sexual appetites. Lust is never satisfied. We try to fill up the hole with the lust of the eye or material possessions. We tell ourselves, if I had enough money I would be happy. We also try to fill up the hole with the pride of life or anything that feeds our egos. We are always looking for something that will give our self-esteem a boost, something to make us feel important.

If these do not bring the self-gratification man needs he will turn to alcohol and drugs, all the while sinking farther and farther into the mire of moral decadence. We have all seen this same thing happen to our friends, neighbors, and family. If we are honest, it has happened to all of us before we came to know Jesus.

Neil Anderson's definition of sin is "Living your life independent of God". What a profound statement. Haven't most of us done just that? We have lived our lives doing what we wanted to do and going where we wanted to go without consciously asking God what He wants.

In the fall, Adam began living his life independent of God. We come into the world with Adam's sin nature (living our lives independent of God). Satan has done a good job of keeping us blinded to the truth. Since I was saved at an early age, and I did all the "good" things that Christians do, I could not "see" that I was a sinner or that I was sinning. Understanding that sin was living my life independent of God put a whole new perspective on sin for me. I believe the Holy Spirit came to live in me at the time of my salvation. I was not taught the truth of God's Word; therefore, I remained a "spiritual baby" for years. Even later on when I believed I had made Jesus Lord of my life, I still lived most of my life independent of God. I made my decisions based on what "**I**" thought was right. I believed the Holy Spirit in me prompted me to do "good" things, but "**I**" was still making most of my decisions based on what "**I**" wanted to do, without praying about it.

All sin starts in the mind. This is where temptation seeks to form its base of power. When desire has conceived, it gives birth to sin; and sin when it is full-grown brings forth death.[58] The devil (the father of all lies and the accuser of the brethren) plants accusations, doubts, or makes ungodly suggestions in our minds to tempt us to do and say the wrong things. This is why it is so important for us to think on the things that are good, lovely, and of a good report.

We have seen the origin of the human race according to the Bible, the fall of man, and the state of man left to his own devices. When a person is born in the flesh, the natural man is carnal. His soul is made up of his mind, which is like a computer where data has been stored from childhood. His soul is also made up of his emotions, which can be either good or bad. Bad emotions produce works of the flesh, adultery, fornication, uncleanness, licentiousness (sexual immorality), idolatry, sorcery, hatred, contentions (strife), jealousies, outbursts of wrath, selfish ambition, dissensions, heresies, envy, murders, drunkenness, revelries, and the like; of which I tell you beforehand, just as I also told you in time past, that those who practice such things will not inherit the kingdom of God.[59] And lastly, he is made up of his will. Big "**I**" rules and reigns over his life. His nature is selfish, which is the root of all sin.

## To summarize "Who Am I" or who is man:

He is born with a sin nature because of Adam.

He cannot receive the things of God because he is carnal.

He lives in a world under the dominion of Satan.

He is a slave to sin & his five senses. He only believes what he can see, hear, taste, touch, and smell.

He has no peace or fellowship with Father God.

Without being born again, Hell is his final destination. He lives in darkness.

He has a hole inside that only God can fill.

He tries to fill the hole with:
Lust of the Flesh—It is pleasing to the flesh
(eating, drinking, fun, sex)
Lust of the Eye—It looks good—I want it.
Pride of Life—Makes him feel important.

Walking in the flesh produces the fruit of the flesh.

He is in a mess! He cries out, "O wretched man that I am! Who can save me from this body of death?

## <u>PRAISE GOD, JESUS CAN!</u> You must be born again!

# Chapter 10

## HOW CAN A PERSON BE "BORN AGAIN"?

W e have talked about the natural man, the carnal man, the man of flesh or before we are born again, the old man. We have seen man left to his own devices without any godly counsel usually means living a corrupt, evil, or perverted lifestyle orchestrated by our arch enemy, Satan. Man is in a mess controlled by his fleshly, carnal, natural mind, emotions, and will. He is living under the law. He has no peace, and he is on his way to everlasting damnation, afraid of death and dying. This is where many have found themselves. The only solution is to be born again. Therefore, "How can a person become born again?"

What do Christians mean when they talk of being born again? Surprisingly enough, you are not the first person to ask. John 3:2 Nicodemus asked Jesus, "Rabbi, we know that You are a teacher come from God; for no one can do these signs that You do unless God is with him." Jesus answered and said to him, "Most assuredly, I say to you, unless one is born again, he cannot see the kingdom of God." Nicodemus said to Him, "How can a man be born when he is old? Can he enter a second time into his mother's womb and be born?" Jesus answered, "Most assuredly, I say to you, unless one is born of water and the Spirit, he cannot enter the kingdom of God. That which is born of the flesh is flesh, and that which is born of the Spirit is spirit. Do not marvel that I said to you, 'You must be born again.' The wind blows where it wishes, and you hear the sound of it, but cannot tell where it comes from and where it goes. So is everyone who is born of the Spirit."

Let's examine some of the common terms associated with being born again or words that Christians use interchangeably when saying a person has been born again. They talk of being saved or being rescued from destruction. It also means being rescued from the way they used to be or rescued from spending eternity in Hell. Another term Christians use is converted. This means they were following their natural inclination of sinning, and now they have decided to follow God. They talk of being reconciled to God, which means to become friends or live in harmony with God again; they are brought back into fellowship with God. Some say they have been regenerated. By this they mean their thought pattern has been reformed; to change radically for the better; or restored to original strength and properties. Christians also say they have been redeemed. When they are redeemed they are bought back. For example, a man owned something but lost possession of it. To get it back a ransom or price had to be paid. In this case man lost his right standing with God through sin. To be reunited with God, a ransom has to be paid.

**Being born again literally means to be begotten from above or from God the Father.**

Now that we have established what being born again means, we must ask ourselves "How can this happen?" We just read, "The wind blows where it wishes, and you hear the sound of it, but cannot tell where it comes from and where it goes. So is everyone who is born of the Spirit." In natural childbirth we know that a seed must be planted in fertile soil. It is nourished until the time of delivery. A child has no knowledge of being in the womb. Most people are conscious of few things before they were three years old. So it is with the rebirth. In James 1:18 we read, "Of His own will He brought us forth by the word of truth, that we might be a kind of first fruits of His creatures." Again in 1 Peter 1:23 the Bible says, "We are born again, not of corruptible seed but incorruptible, through the word of God which lives and abides forever".

The seed that is planted is not of corruptible seed. This seed is by no human generation, or earthly means, but is incorruptible. It is a divine and heavenly principle which is not liable to decay or to be affected by the changes and chances to which all sublunary (all things under the moon) things are exposed. This incorruptible seed is the word of truth. What truth? The Bible says "Sanctify them by your truth. Your word is truth.[60] You shall know the truth, and the truth shall make you free."[61] How then is the seed impregnated? "Faith comes by <u>hearing and hearing</u> comes by the word of God."[62] "I am not ashamed of the gospel of Christ, for it is the power of God to salvation for everyone who believes, for the Jew first and also for the Greek. For in it the righteousness of God is revealed from faith to faith; as it is written, 'The just shall live by faith.'"[63] "Most assuredly, I say to you, he who hears My word and believes in Him who sent Me has everlasting life, and shall not come into judgment, but has passed from death into life."[64]

The truth of the gospel, or good news, is the power of God that he uses to bring men to a saving knowledge of who He is. Salvation, or rebirth, is that for which the natural man has searched to fill the void left in his soul because of Adam's sin and to deliver him from the mess in which he has found himself when left to his own devices. There comes a transformation from God and a renewal in righteousness and true holiness when we are born again or saved. Usually we are as unaware of being born again spiritually as we were unaware of being born again physically, until one day we realize our "want to" has changed. What we used to "want to" do is no longer what we now "want to" do.

Now that we have established the fact that a person can be born again spiritually, you may be asking, "Why would a person want to be born again?" "Assuredly, I say to you, unless you are converted or born again and become as little children, you will by no means enter the kingdom of heaven. Therefore whoever humbles himself as this little child is the greatest in the kingdom of heaven."[65] "For all have sinned, and come short of the glory of God; Being justified freely by his grace through the redemption that is in Christ Jesus: Whom God hath set forth to be a propitiation (an atoning sacrifice) through faith in his blood (believing the blood He shed on the cross was the only sacrifice acceptable to God for sin), to declare his righteousness for the remission (doing away) of sins that are past, through the forbearance (tolerance) of God."[66] Therefore, if we want to enter the kingdom of heaven we must be born again. We have to be sorry that we have sinned and repent.

According to the Mosaic Law almost all things are purified with blood, and without shedding of blood there would be no remission of sins.[67] If Jesus had not been willing to die for our sins, we would have had to pay. Since we would have had to pay with our blood, we would have had to die. A praise course says it so beautifully: "He paid a debt, He did not owe, and I owed a debt I could not pay. I needed someone to take my sins away!" Only a blood sacrifice will redeem us from our sins. "Now I sing a brand new song, amazing grace; He paid the debt that I could never pay!"

Since our own righteousness is as filthy rags, who then can be born again? This means we can never be good enough to get to heaven.[68] We cry out, "Oh wretched man that I am! Who will deliver me from this body of death?"[69] Without the God of the Bible there is no one. Jesus says "Most assuredly, I say to you, unless one is born again, he cannot see the kingdom of God." Therefore if anyone wants to see the kingdom of God, they must be born again to have eternal life.[70] "This is the will of God who sent Jesus that everyone who sees the Son and believes in Him may have eternal life; and God will raise him up at the last day."[71] "God so loved the world that He gave His only begotten Son so that no one should perish but have everlasting life."[72] After Jesus raised Lazarus from the dead; Jesus said to Martha, "I am the resurrection and the life. He who believes in Me, though he may die, he shall live. And whoever lives and believes in Me shall never die. Do you believe this?"[73] If a person believes and receives Jesus, He gives to them the right to become children of God, to all those who believe in His name: who are born, not of blood, nor of the will of the flesh, nor of the will of man, but of God.[74] "Whoever shall call upon the name of the Lord shall be saved. How shall they call on him in whom they have not believed? And how shall they believe in him of whom they have not heard? And how shall they hear without a preacher? And how shall they preach, except they be sent? As it is written, how beautiful are the feet of them that preach the gospel of peace, and bring glad tidings of good things! But they have not all obeyed the gospel. So then faith comes by hearing, and hearing by the word of God."[75] "Without faith it is impossible to please Him, for he who comes to God must believe that He is, and that He rewards those who diligently seek Him."[76]

When we hear the good news of who Jesus is, believe in our heart that He arose from the dead, are sorry for things we have done in violation of His will and confess with our mouth He is the Son of God, and invite Him to take control of our lives, we have done all we can do to be born again. No amount of money, right living, morals, or giving can bring salvation to a person. Our salvation, or being born again, only comes by the grace of God and the blood of Jesus Christ. He brings about our salvation when we invite Him to do so.

When a person is born again, his spirit man becomes alive as the Holy Spirit takes residence. By this one act of obedience, so many things happen. Usually the first thing an adult "feels" is a sense of being at peace. That's because he is reconciled to God the Father. His relationship has been restored with Him. He has been redeemed or bought back by Jesus. His sins are now forgiven. He might feel as if a weight has been lifted. Man is now justified, or pronounced free, from guilt or sin. It's just as if he had never sinned. Many people know the day they walked the aisle and made a public profession of their faith, but usually the seed was planted long before they were made aware of it being planted. After a person is born again, then the process of sanctification begins. This is a work of the Holy Spirit who now resides in the heart of the born again man. Very subtly and subconsciously the Holy Spirit begins to change us from the inside out.

"Therefore, if anyone is in Christ, he is a new creation; old things have passed away; behold, all things have become new. For He made Him who knew no sin to be sin for us, that we might become the righteousness of God in Him."[77] "And you He made alive, who were dead in trespasses and sins, in which you once walked according to the course of this world, according to the prince of the power of the air, the spirit who now works in the sons of disobedience, among whom also we all once conducted ourselves in the lusts of our flesh, fulfilling the desires of the flesh and of the mind, and were by nature children of wrath, just as the others."[78]

After a man is born again, he is to put off concerning his former conduct, the old man which grows corrupt according to its deceitful lusts, and be renewed in the spirit of his mind. He is to put on the new man, who was created according to the likeness of God, in true righteousness and holiness.[79]

So far, we have established the fact that without being born again man is dead in his trespasses and sins. It is God's will that no man should perish but have everlasting life. We have seen without faith it is impossible to please God. We have seen that if we receive Jesus, we are given the power to become the sons of God. We know that faith comes from hearing the Word of God, and we know someone has to bring us that message.

When the spirit within a man hears the words of salvation, he feels a tugging in his heart; he longs to return to Father God who sent him to live inside of the man. I believe that just like the salmon, there is that innate nature in man to return to that from which he originated. So the spirit within recognizes the truth. This is what brings conviction to a person. At this point man realizes he needs a savior to save him from his sins. So he cries out, what must I do to be saved?

Now when they heard this, they were cut to the heart, and said to Peter and the rest of the apostles, "Men and brethren, what shall we do? Then Peter said to them, "Repent, and let every one of you be baptized in the name of Jesus Christ for the remission of sins; and you shall receive the gift of the Holy Spirit. For the promise is to you and to your children, and to all who are afar off, as many as the Lord our God will call."[80] Then those who gladly received his word were baptized; Repent therefore and be converted, that your sins may be blotted out, so that times of refreshing may come from the presence of the Lord.[81]

When a person repents he feels regret and sorrow for the way he has lived to the degree that he no longer wants to live that way anymore. He realizes that the big "I" has ruled and reigned in his heart and brought about the condition in which he now finds himself. He has been going his own way and doing his own thing without regards to what God the Father who created him, wants him to do.

Baptize comes from the Greek word "baptize," which means to make whelmed (i.e. fully wet or submerged). He who believes and is baptized will be saved; but he who does not believe will be condemned.[82] Different denominations have different interpretations of baptism. Some say "Baptism is an outward expression of an inward conviction." Some say "Baptism doesn't save you; it is an act of obedience." Therefore, it makes no difference if you are sprinkled or submerged.

I agree with both statements to a degree; however, when it is said it usually sounds as if they think baptism is unimportant. I think nothing should take away from the importance of being baptized, and more emphasis should be put on the fact that it is symbolic of our old man dying and being raised a new creature in Christ Jesus. If the word says to believe and be baptized to be saved, to receive eternal life, and the gift of the Holy Spirit, why argue about being baptized? Just do it! If you have surrendered your will to the Lordship of Jesus Christ, you will not have a problem being baptized.

"What shall we say then? Shall we continue in sin that grace may abound? Certainly not! How shall we who died to sin live any longer in it? Or do you not know that as many of us as were baptized into Christ Jesus were baptized into His death? Therefore we were buried with Him through baptism into death, that just as Christ was raised from the dead by the glory of the Father, even so we also should walk in newness of life. For if we have been united together in the likeness of His death, certainly we also shall be in the likeness of His resurrection, knowing this, that our old man was crucified with Him, that the body of sin might be done away with, that we should no longer be slaves of sin. For he who has died has been freed from sin. Now if we died with Christ, we believe that we shall also live with Him, knowing that Christ, having been raised from the dead, dies no more. Death no longer has dominion over Him. For the death that He died, He died to sin once for all; but the life that He lives, He lives to God. Likewise you also, reckon yourselves to be dead indeed to sin, but alive to God in Christ Jesus our Lord."[83] This stresses the importance of being baptized. It symbolizes our old man being crucified; and now we arise as a new creature, dead to sin but alive to Christ.

If you confess with your mouth the Lord Jesus and believe in your heart that God has raised Him from the dead, you will be saved. "For with the heart one believes unto righteousness and with the mouth confession is made unto salvation."[84] When we confess something, we admit, or acknowledge, we have done wrong. In the instance of salvation, a person admits he is a sinner in need of a savior and acknowledges that Jesus is the only way to be reconciled to God the Father.

Up to this point man has heard the word, believed it, been convicted, repented, confessed Jesus as Lord, and been baptized; somewhere along the way he became born again. Proving the scripture that says, "The wind blows where it wishes, and you hear the sound of it, but cannot tell where it comes from and where it goes. So is everyone who is born of the Spirit."

After a man is born again, he is to put off, concerning his former conduct, the old man which grows corrupt according to the deceitful lusts, be renewed in the spirit of his mind, and put on the new man who was created according to God in true righteousness and holiness. The Grace of God now comes upon this born again man!

"But God, who is rich in mercy, because of His great love with which He loved us, even when we were dead in trespasses, made us alive together with Christ (by grace you have been saved), and raised us up together, and made us sit together in the heavenly places in Christ Jesus, that in the ages to come He might show the exceeding riches of His grace in His kindness toward us in Christ Jesus. For by grace you have been saved through faith, and that not of yourselves; it is the gift of God, not of works, lest anyone should boast. We are His workmanship, created in Christ Jesus for good works, which God prepared beforehand that we should walk in them."[85]

In answering the question "How can a person be born again?" you should see that the natural, carnal man needs to be born again to be forgiven of his sins and receive eternal life. As he hears the word proclaimed, he believes, he repents, he confesses he is a sinner in need of a savior and believes Jesus is the only way to the Father. He is baptized in obedience to the Word of God. God saves him through His matchless grace. Man becomes a new creature in Christ. It may or may not be a bolt of lightening experience. Usually it is rather like being born in the natural. You don't remember being born by your mother, but you realize at some point you were born because you are alive. Once you are born again, one day you will <u>know</u> your "want to's" have changed. You will realize you are at peace. You will be able to understand spiritual things you have never understood before and you will realize you have been born again!

Behold old things are washed away, all things have become new!

Praise the Lord!

# Chapter 11

## WHO IS THIS NEW CREATURE?

(Or our spirit Man)

W hen you comprehend what takes place the moment a person is born again and begin to understand this new creature, it should change your outlook on everything.

In the past two chapters we discussed what happens to the carnal, or natural, man when left to his own devices. He desperately needs a savior. We then talked about what it means to be born again. So today we want to take a good look at this new creation. To review the last chapter, we see when a person receives Jesus Christ as his Savior:

- He is born again.

- He is a new creation.

- By Grace His sins are forgiven as far as the east is from the west.

- He has entered into eternal life.

- The Lord of His life is God the Father, God the Son and God the Holy Spirit.

- He is made at peace with God the Father.

- Heaven is now his final destination.

- He has been translated from darkness and has entered in the kingdom of God's dear Son.

- He should now live by faith instead of making decisions based on his five senses.

- He has FREEDOM!!

- The promises of God are to the new man, yes and amen (so be it).

Let's take a look at what else happens the moment we are born again! As we look at the Scriptures we see, when man is born again he is put back into right standing with God that Adam had enjoyed.

## Adam and Eve no longer lived by faith in God. The new man is to live by faith.

When Adam fell, he had to rely on his knowledge based on his five senses or his intellectual ability. Adam no longer enjoyed intimate fellowship with God. He was banished from the Garden of Eden and God's presence when he sinned. Because of the sin nature we inherited from Adam, the natural man knows something about God but he doesn't know God.

Adam and Eve had eaten from the knowledge of the tree of good and evil and their judgment on how to live was based on their five senses: hear, see, taste, touch, and smell. Adam became a victim of the intellectual world.

When man becomes a new creature in Christ, he begins to walk by faith. "For we walk by faith, not by sight."[86]

## Adam and Eve no longer had an intimate relationship with God. The new man has this privilege.

In our unregenerate state, we know something about God, but we don't know God because we have no relationship with Him. But the new creature has been put back in right standing with God. "Therefore, if anyone is in Christ, he is a new creation; old things have passed away; behold, all things have become new. Now all things are of God, who has reconciled us to Himself through Jesus Christ."[87]

## The old man's fear has been replaced by faith.

The old man worried and lived in fear of failing. We are no longer afraid because we know our heavenly Father will take care of us. "For as many as are led by the Spirit of God, these are sons of God. You did not receive the spirit of bondage again to fear, but you received the Spirit of adoption by whom we cry out, "Abba, Father."[88]

## Death is no longer to be feared by the new man.

The old man was in bondage and afraid of death because of the choices he had made in life. He would have been separated from God, if he had died. We are going to a better place when we die. "As much then as the children have partaken of flesh and blood, Jesus Himself likewise shared in the same, that through death He might destroy him who had the power of death, that is, the devil, and releases those who through fear of death were all their lifetime subject to bondage."[89]

## Anger and depression were emotions with which Adam had to deal with because of sin.

Now by God's grace we can put off this old way of thinking, acting, or reacting. "You were taught, with regard to your former way of life, to put off your old self, which is being corrupted by its deceitful desires; to be made new in the attitude of your minds; and to put on the new self, created to be like God in true righteousness and holiness."[90]

## Adam felt rejection and the new man feels acceptance.

The old man has a great need to be accepted, to feel assured and have self confidence; he has a need to belong. The new man is accepted and loved by God. When we grow into awareness of who we are, we have a sense of belonging that nothing can erase. The Bible supports this thought in the following: "Blessed be the God and Father of our Lord Jesus Christ, who has blessed us with every spiritual blessing in the heavenly places in Christ, just as He chose us in Him before the foundation of the world, that we should be holy and without blame before Him in love, having predestined us to adoption as sons by Jesus Christ to Himself, according to the good pleasure of His will, to the praise of the glory of His grace, by which He made us accepted in the Beloved."[91]

## Adam's Innocence was replaced by guilt and shame. The new man is innocent.

No matter what we have done in the past it will be removed from us when we stand before Him on Judgment Day. "Therefore you do not lack any spiritual gift as you eagerly wait for our Lord Jesus Christ to be revealed. He will keep you strong to the end, so that you will be blameless on the day of our Lord Jesus Christ."[92]

## Adam's authority was replaced by weakness and helplessness.

The new creature is no longer weak or helpless. He is no longer in bondage to Satan, he is free! This new man has the strength and power of Almighty God at his disposal. "Those who wait on the Lord, shall renew their strength; they shall mount up with wings like eagles, they shall run and not be weary, they shall walk and not faint."[93]

A person's "old" man has ruled so long and Satan has been in control of his life so long, that unless he gets a good understanding of his new position and the authority he now has over Satan, his spirit man is not going to grow and he will not have a victorious life. Man, the new creature, is now restored to the original position God intended which Adam enjoyed in the Garden of Eden.

## With that thought in mind, let us take a look at the spirit of man.

We are told the new creature's spirit is made up of his renewed conscience, his intuition or discernment, and his capacity for worship. Let's look at his conscience. Hebrews 9:12-14 states, God cleanses the new creature's conscience. Wow, how great is that!!

"For not with the blood of goats and calves, but with His own blood He entered the Most Holy Place once for all, having obtained eternal redemption. If the blood of bulls and goats and the ashes of a heifer, sprinkling the unclean, sanctifies for the purifying of the flesh, how much more shall the blood of Christ, who through the eternal Spirit offered

Himself without spot to God, cleanse your conscience from dead works to serve the living God?"[94] "We are not to be conformed to this world but we are to be transformed by the renewing of our minds that we may prove what is good and acceptable and the perfect will of God." [95] As our mind is transformed our spirit man grows and the ways of the flesh are put to death.

Intuition or discernment is the power, or faculty of attaining direct knowledge or cognition without rational thought or inference. The man without the Spirit does not accept the things that come from the Spirit of God, for they are foolishness to him, and he cannot understand them, because they are spiritually discerned.[96] This new creature now has intuition or discernment he lacked before he was born again.

The natural man does not have the desire to worship God. It is not normal for the natural man to worship God. Only the Holy Spirit in man can worship God. Natural man brings forth curses; the new creature brings forth praise! God is spirit, and his worshipers must worship in spirit and in truth."[97] Therefore I make known to you that no one speaking by the Spirit of God calls Jesus accursed, and no one can say that Jesus is Lord except by the Holy Spirit.[98] With the tongue we praise our Lord and Father, and with it we curse men, who have been made in God's likeness. Out of the same mouth come praise and cursing. My brothers, this should not be. Can both fresh water and salt water flow from the same spring? My brothers, can a fig tree bear olives, or a grapevine bear figs? Neither can a salt spring produce fresh water.[99] Our new creature now has the ability to praise God.

As we have our mind renewed to the word of God, our conscience becomes a good guide to direct us in the way we should go. Our intuition or our discernment is sharpened as the Holy Spirit grows in us. As we clean up our minds and our emotions, learn to die to self, and learn to rule our tongue we have the capacity to worship God. Sweet and bitter water cannot come out of the same fountain so neither can praises to God and curses.

Just as it is imperative for a new baby to be fed to grow into manhood, so, the newborn creature must be fed the Word of God to grow into maturity. Just as a baby is taught to walk, so our new creature must learn to walk in the spirit. Just as a baby is taught to be productive, so our new creature must be taught to be productive.

This new creation now has to grow in maturity. He will produce the fruit of the Spirit which is love, joy, peace, longsuffering, kindness, goodness, faithfulness, gentleness, and self-control as he trusts and obeys the Father.[100]

Let us go to the Word of God to see a few more things that happen when a person is born again and becomes a new creature:

Ephesians 1:3 "Blessed be the God and Father of our Lord Jesus Christ, who has blessed us with every spiritual blessing in the heavenly places in Christ."

Verse 4 "He chose us in Him before the foundation of the world, that we should be holy and without blame before Him in love."

Verse 5 "He predestined us to adoption as sons by Jesus Christ to Himself, according to the good pleasure of His will."

Verse 6 To the praise of the glory of His grace, by which He made us accepted in the Beloved.

Verse 7 "In Him we have redemption through His blood, the forgiveness of sins, according to the riches of His grace."

Verse 8 "Which He made to abound toward us in all wisdom and prudence."

Verse 9-11 "In Him also we have obtained an inheritance, having made known to us the mystery of His will, according to His good pleasure which He purposed in Himself, being predestined according to the purpose of Him who works all things according to the counsel of His will, that we who first trusted in Christ should be to the praise of His glory"

Verse 13 "In Him you also trusted, after you heard the word of truth, the gospel of your salvation; in whom also, having believed, you were sealed with the Holy Spirit of promise."

Ephesians 2:11 But now in Christ Jesus, you who once were far off have been brought near by the blood of Christ."

Verse 18 "Through Him we both have access by one Spirit to the Father."

Verse 19 "Now, therefore, you are no longer strangers and foreigners, but fellow citizens with the saints and members of the household of God."

Verse 20 "Having been built on the foundation of the apostles and prophets, Jesus Christ Himself being the chief cornerstone"

Verse 21-22 "In whom the whole building, being fitted together, grows into a holy temple in the Lord, in whom you also are being built together for a dwelling place of God in the Spirit."

Romans 5:9 "Much more then, having now been justified by His blood, we shall be saved from wrath through Him."

Verse 10 "If when we were enemies we were reconciled to God through the death of His Son, much more; having been reconciled, we shall be saved by His life."

Verse 18 "If by the one man's offense death reigned through the one, much more those who receive abundance of grace and of the gift of righteousness will reign in life through the One, Jesus Christ."

Verse 19 "As by one man's disobedience many were made sinners, so also by one Man's obedience many will be made righteous."

Romans 6:11 "Likewise you also, reckon yourselves to be dead indeed to sin, but alive to God in Christ Jesus our Lord."

Verse 14 "Sin shall not have dominion over you, for you are not under law but under grace."

Verse 15 "What then? Shall we sin because we are not under law but under grace? Certainly not! Sin is no longer our master."

Verse 23 "The wages of sin is death, but the gift of God is eternal life in Christ Jesus our Lord."

Romans 8:1 "There is therefore now no condemnation to those who are in Christ Jesus, who do not walk according to the flesh, but according to the Spirit."

Verse 4 "The righteous requirement of the law might be fulfilled in us who do not walk according to the flesh but according to the Spirit. For those who live according to the flesh set their minds on the things of the flesh, but those who live according to the Spirit, the things of the Spirit. To be carnally minded is death, but to be spiritually minded is life and peace."

## Wow! Is this good or what?

Let us look at one more important Scripture now that we are new creatures in Christ:

Acts 10:34 "Of a truth I perceive that God is no respecter of persons."

What does that mean? It means God loves me as much as he loves any other Christian; And He loves me more than those in the world so I figure, "This makes me as good as the best and better than the rest!"!! **Hallelujah!** If this is not enough to convince you that you are someone special, read the following to see what the Bible says about this new creature.

## "Who Am I?"

I am the salt of the earth (Matthew 5:13)

I am the light of the world (Matthew 5:14)

I am a child of God (John 1:12)

I am part of the true vine, a channel of Christ's life (John 15:1, 5)

I am Christ's friend (John 15:15)

I am chosen and appointed by Christ to bear His fruit (John 15:16)

I am a slave of righteousness (Romans. 6:18)

I am enslaved to God (Romans 6:22)

I am a son of God; God is spiritually my Father (Romans 8:14, 15 Gal. 3:26; 4:6)

I am a joint heir with Christ, sharing His inheritance with Him (Romans. 8:17)

I am a temple, a dwelling place, of God; His spirit and His life dwells in me (1 Corinthians 3:16; 6:19)

I am united to the Lord and am one spirit with Him (1 Corinthians 6:17)

I am a member of Christ's body (1 Corinthians 12:27; Ephesians 5:30)

I am a new creation (2 Corinthians 5:17)

I am reconciled to God and am a minister of reconciliation (2 Corinthians 5:18, 19)

I am a son of God and one in Christ (Galatians 3:26, 28).

I am an heir of God since I am a son of God (Galatians 4:6, 7)

I am a saint (Ephesians 1:1; 1 Corinthians 1:2; Philippians 1:1; Colossians 1:2)

I am God's workmanship, His handiwork, born anew in Christ to do His work (Ephesians 2:10)

I am a fellow citizen with the rest of God's family (Ephesians 2:19)

I am a prisoner of Christ (Ephesians. 3:1; 4:1)

I am righteous and holy (Ephesians 4:24)

I am a citizen of heaven, seated in heaven right now (Philippians 3:20; Ephesians 2:6)

I am hidden with Christ in God (Colossians 3:3)

I am an expression of the life of Christ because He is my life (Colossians 3:4)

I am chosen of God, holy and dearly loved (Colossians 3:12; 1 Thessalonians 1:4).

I am a son of light and not of darkness (1 Thessalonians 5:5)

I am a holy partaker of a heavenly calling (Hebrews 3:1).

I am a partaker of Christ; I share in His life (Hebrews 3:14).

I am one of God's living stones, being built up in Christ as a spiritual house (1Peter 2:5).

I am a member of a chosen race, a royal priesthood, a holy nation, a people for God's own possession (1 Peter 2:9, 10).

I am an alien and stranger to this world in which I temporarily live (1 Peter 2:11).

I am an enemy of the devil (1 Peter 5:8).

I am a child of God and I will resemble Christ when He returns (1 John 3:1, 2).

I am born of God, and the evil one, the devil, cannot touch me (1 John 5:18).

I am not the great "I AM" (Exodus 3:14; John 8:24, 28, 58), but by the grace of God, I am what I am. (1 Corinthians 15:10).

Since I am in Christ, by the grace of God . . . .

I have been justified, completely forgiven and made righteous (Romans 5:1)

I died with Christ and died to the power of sin's rule over my life. (Romans 5:1)

I am free forever from condemnation (Romans 8:1)

I have been placed into Christ by God's doing (1 Corinthians 1:30)

I have received the Spirit of God into my life that I might know the things freely given to me by God (1 Corinthians 2:12)

I have been given the mind of Christ (1Corinthians 2:16)

I have been bought with a price: I am not my own; I belong to God (1 Corinthians 6:19-20)

I have been established, anointed and sealed by God in Christ, and I have been given the Holy Spirit as a pledge guaranteeing my inheritance to come (2 Corinthians 1:21; Ephesians 1:13, 14)

Since I have died, I no longer live for myself, but for Christ (2 Corinthians 5:14, 15)

I have been made righteous (2 Corinthians 5:21).

I have been crucified with Christ and it is no longer I who live, but Christ lives in me. The life I am now living is Christ's life (Galatians 2:20)

I have been blessed with every spiritual blessing (Ephesians 1:3)

I was chosen in Christ before the foundation of the world to be holy and am without blame before Him (Ephesians 1)

I was predestined, determined by God, to be adopted as God's son (Ephesians 1:5)

I have been redeemed and forgiven, and I am a recipient of his lavish grace and-

I have been made alive together with Christ (Ephesians 2:5)

I have been raised up and seated with Christ in heaven (Ephesians 2:6)

I have direct access to God through the Spirit (Ephesians 2:18)

I may approach God with boldness, freedom and confidence (Ephesians 3:12)

I have been rescued from the dominion of Satan's rule and transferred to the kingdom of Christ (Colossians 1:13)

I have been redeemed and forgiven of all my sins. The debt against me has been canceled (Colossians 1:14)

Christ Himself is in me (Colossians 1:27)

I am firmly rooted in Christ and am now being built in Him (Colossians 2:7)

I have been spiritually circumcised; my old unregenerate nature has been removed (Colossians. 2:11)

I have been made complete in Christ (Colossians 2:10)

I have been buried, raised and made alive with Christ (Colossians. 2:12, 13)

I died with Christ, and I have been raised up with Christ; my life is now hidden with Christ in God. Christ is now my life (Colossians. 3:1-4)

I have been given a spirit of power, love and self-discipline (2 Timothy 1:7)

I have been saved and set apart according to God's doing (2 Timothy. 1:9; Titus 3:5)

Because I am sanctified and am one with the Sanctifier, He is not ashamed to call me brother (Hebrews 2:11)

I have a right to come boldly before the throne of God to find mercy and grace in time of need (Hebrews 4:16)

I have been given exceedingly great and precious promises by God by which I am a partaker of God's divine nature (2 Peter 1:4)

Everything we have studied today is what happens when we surrender the big "I" who rules and reigns in our human nature to the Lordship of Jesus Christ! When we grasp the fact of who this new creature is that dwells within us, we will never feel inferior or insignificant again. We just have to believe that what the Word of God says about us is true! The benefits are monumental!!!

"I may never have a big ministry, I may never have a big business and I may never be well recognized in the arenas of man but I will never be insignificant. I am the one He loves, I am the one He died for, and I am the one He longs for. I am the one He waits for. Therefore, I can never be insignificant again and neither can you." This is quoted from Mike Bickle's book, "The Pleasures of Loving God."

# Chapter 12

## HOW DO I PRAY AND MEDITATE?

T he most important thing in learning to pray and meditate is to understand the importance of prayer. As we see the importance of prayer and meditation it should help us "will" to set aside a time that we can do the most important thing that God has called us to do.

Have you ever noticed when we are trying to have time alone with the Lord, how often we are interrupted? The phone will ring; you have company; someone will come to the door; we have an appointment that we must keep or we oversleep and don't have time! I always have prayed at meals and I pray little prayers off and on all day. When I am alone I often pray: walking, driving, before I go to sleep (however sometimes I am so sleepy, I go to sleep while I am praying)! I have tried getting up to pray before I went to work but to do that I had to get up at 6:00 AM and I couldn't stay alert. Sometimes I could focus, but more often than not my mind would drift. My husband always blessed our food before meals and now that I am alone, all of a sudden I will realize I have not even said a blessing!

What I am trying to say is, "We have an enemy who does not want us to pray." Praying and meditating on the Word of God should be a priority in our lives. Oh, when we get in a "jam" we know where to go; but, if we are to have a deeper, more meaningful relationship with the Lord, all of us need to work on our prayer life. With that in mind, let's take a look at prayer and meditation.

Many new converts think you must have some great oratorical ability to pray to God. They feel someone will judge them for not saying the "right" words. When you accept Jesus as your Savior this gives you access to the throne room of God. You can now approach the heavenly Father just as you would your earthly Father. If you talk to your earthly father in King James English, by all means pray that way. If you talk like New Yorkers then pray like New Yorkers. If you are a southerner like me, He doesn't mind my drawl; He rather likes my accent when I pray. Even if I use colloquialisms, He understands. In other words, it really doesn't matter how you pray. He is your heavenly Father and He loves you and wants you to talk to Him. Praying is just talking to your heavenly Father as you would your earthly Father.

Prayer is a means we use to approach God in word or thought to give thanks, praise, or to worship; it means to make an entreaty, petition or an earnest request on behalf of ourselves or someone else. I asked my heavenly Father once, "If You know what I need before I pray, why do I need to pray?" His answer was so simple, yet so profound. If I did not ask Him to do something, I would not know He answered. His answers are sometimes "yes," sometimes "no," sometimes "wait," and sometimes it seems as though He hasn't even heard us. I have come to call this "test time". You pray and pray, plead, expect an answer and nothing!! None of your friends, family, no preacher or anyone else can help you! Just as you are on the brink of doom with nowhere to turn, there comes a whisper, "Are you going to trust me, no matter what?" As you surrender, the answer comes. You have aced the test!! When we pray and God answers, our faith grows. We learn about the characteristics of our God and we learn so much about ourselves. Prayer is the key to the Kingdom of God!

Jesus' disciples heard him pray and saw the results. On one occasion they had seen him bless the two loaves and five fish and saw Him feed the five thousand. They knew He had connections with the Father as they were present when all the miracles took place. They wanted to be able to pray as John and Jesus prayed. In Luke 11:1 we read, Now it came to pass, as He was praying in a certain place, when He ceased, that one of His disciples said to Him, "Lord, teach us to pray, as John also taught his disciples." So He said to them, "When you pray, say:

> Our Father, which art in heaven,
> Hallowed be Your name.
> Your kingdom come.
> Your will be done
> On earth as it is in heaven.
> Give us this day our daily bread.
> And forgive us our debts or trespasses,
> For we also forgive our debtors or those who trespass against us.
> And do not lead us into temptation,

But deliver us from the evil one."
For Yours is the kingdom and the power
and the glory for ever and ever. Amen.

Taking this as our model prayer let's give it some thought. Prayer begins by worshipping the Father.

**Our father, which art in heaven.** In this phrase we are proclaiming He is "our" father and denoting that this father is the one in heaven.

**Hallowed be Your name.** We are requesting and praying that God's name be regarded with great respect and reverence.

**Your kingdom come.** We are asking God to be the King and ruler of our hearts. Only after He resides as King in our lives can we share the good news, so that the Kingdom of God might enter into the hearts of others.

**Your will be done.** His word is His will.

**On earth as it is in heaven.** We must obey His Word to see that His will is carried out in our lives. Everything we undertake should be taken to the Lord in prayer asking Him to give us His will and His wisdom. As each step is prayed for and is shown to be clearly the will of God. Then we can expect to see miracles take place.

**Give us this day our daily bread.** Effective prayer means daily contact with the Lord. God wants us daily to be in utter dependence on Him. He wants us to daily feel the need of the strength of His presence and sustaining power.

**And forgive us our debts or trespasses.** In our daily lives, we break moral or social laws; we say or do something to offend someone and at times we are unaware of the effect our actions have on someone else, so we need for God to forgive us. We might have hurt others, but God is the one we sin against when we don't live up to what we should be as an imitator of Jesus, so we need Him to forgive us.

**As we forgive our debtors or those who trespass against us.** We are asking God to forgive us based on how we forgive others. Oh my!

> "For if you forgive men their trespasses, your heavenly Father will also forgive you. But if you do not forgive men their trespasses, neither will your Father forgive your trespasses.[101]

**And do not lead us into temptation.** We all must face temptation, so we need to anticipate it ahead of time and be prepared, so the Devil will not be able to blindside us. The most subtle temptation involves human pride and ambition.

**But deliver us from the evil one.** The devil roams about seeking whom he may devour. So we must be on guard and pray for God's protection.

**For Yours is the kingdom and the power and the glory forever. Amen.** Just as prayer begins with worship it also ends with worship.

### Jesus teaches us how not to pray.

> Matthew 6:5-7 "And when you pray, you shall not be like the hypocrites. For they love to pray standing in the synagogues and on the corners of the streets, that they may be seen by men. Assuredly, I say to you, they have their reward. But you, when you pray, go into your room, and when you have shut your door, pray to your Father who is in the secret place; and your Father who sees in secret will reward you openly. And when you pray, do not use vain repetitions as the heathen do. For they think that they will be heard for their many words."

> "Therefore do not be like them. For your Father knows the things you have need of before you ask Him."[102]

This does not mean we are not to pray where others can hear us. We are not to pray to be seen of men or to show how spiritual we might be. Vain repetitions mean saying the same thing over and over. God is not hard of hearing nor does He have dementia. Many times I have prayed about a situation over and over and have found myself worrying instead of trusting God, who told us to cast our cares on Him. When you cast something, you get rid of it. If we give the problem to Him, He can't fix it if we keep snatching it back.

### Why Pray?

> Philippians 4:6 says "Be anxious for nothing, but in everything by prayer and supplication (ask humbly and earnestly), with thanksgiving, let your requests be made known to God; and the peace of God, which surpasses all understanding, will guard your hearts and minds through Christ Jesus."

Once in my life when we had a bad report from the doctor, worry jumped on me and almost won the battle. Along came fear and anxiety taunting me. As soon as I realized I had been attacked, I shot up a quick prayer right in the middle of my waiting on customers at work. "God, I know worry is a lack of trusting You in this situation but if You don't help me, I have had it. I need Your help!" God sent an angel in the form of a customer, who told me in the course of our conversation; "I was so afraid. I would worry and pray and pray and worry. After putting up with me for a few minutes, God told me if you are going to worry, why pray? And if you are going to pray, why worry?" I almost said out loud, "Aye, Aye Sir!" I got the message, He helped me not worry. For over a week, we did not know what the outcome would be but I knew it was in His capable hands. Thank God He answers prayer!

When we pray we are to thank Him for what is happening in our lives because this is His will for us. Rejoice always, pray without ceasing, and in everything give thanks; for this is the will of God in Christ Jesus for you. [103]

Matthew 7:7 "Ask, and it will be given to you; seek, and you will find; knock, and it will be opened to you. Everyone who asks receives, and he who seeks finds, and to him who knocks it will be opened. Or what man is there among you who, if his son asks for bread, will give him a stone? Or if he asks for a fish, will he give him a serpent? If you then, being evil, know how to give good gifts to your children, how much more will your Father who is in heaven give good things to those who ask Him!" When we pray to the Father asking, seeking, or knocking, our prayers will be answered.

Matthew 26:41 "Watch and pray, lest you enter into temptation. The spirit indeed is willing, but the flesh is weak."

Luke 21:36 "Watch therefore, and pray always that you may be counted worthy to escape all these things that will come to pass and to stand before the Son of Man." When we pray we need to ask to be counted worthy to escape all that is coming upon the earth.

Luke 12:32-47 "Jesus said "Do not fear, little flock, for it is your Father's good pleasure to give you the kingdom. Sell what you have and give alms; provide yourselves money bags which do not grow old, a treasure in the heavens that does not fail, where no thief approaches nor moth destroys. For where your treasure is, there your heart will be also."

"Let your waist be girded and your lamps burning; and you yourselves be like men who wait for their master, when he will return from the wedding, that when he comes and knocks they may open to him immediately. Blessed are those servants whom the master, when he comes, will find watching. Assuredly, I say to you that he will gird himself and have them sit down to eat, and will come and serve them. And if he should come in the second watch, or come in the third watch, and find them so, blessed are those servants. But know this, that if the master of the house had known what hour the thief would come, he would have watched and not allowed his house to be broken into. Therefore you also be ready, for the Son of Man is coming at an hour you do not expect."

Then Peter said to Him, "Lord, do You speak this parable only to us, or to all people?"

And the Lord said, "Who then is that faithful and wise steward, whom his master will make ruler over his household, to give them their portion of food in due season? Blessed is that servant whom his master will find so doing when he comes. Truly, I say to you that he will make him ruler over all that he has. But if that servant says in his heart, 'My master is delaying his coming,' and begins to beat the male and female servants, and to eat and drink and be drunk, the master of that servant will come on a day when he is not looking for him, and at an hour when he is not aware, and will cut him in two and appoint him his portion with the unbelievers. And that servant who knew his master's will, and did not prepare himself or do according to his will, shall be beaten with many stripes.

## When should we pray?

**Always!!** This means to always be in an attitude of prayer; always be ready to lift your needs and those of others to the Lord.

Luke 18:1 "Then He spoke a parable to them, that men always ought to pray and not lose heart."

1 Thessalonians 5:17 "Pray without ceasing, in everything give thanks; for this is the will of God in Christ Jesus for you."

Ephesians 6:18 "Pray always with all prayer and supplication in the Spirit, being watchful to this end with all perseverance and supplication for all the saints."

**When in distress.**

Psalms 118:5 "I called on the LORD in distress; The LORD answered me and set me in a broad place."

**When afflicted.**

James 5:13 "Is anyone among you suffering? Let him pray."

**Pray in Jesus' name.**

Sometimes just saying the name of Jesus brings deliverance and peace.

John 16:23 "And in that day you will ask Me nothing. Most assuredly, I say to you, whatever you ask the Father in My name He will give you. Until now you have asked nothing in My name. Ask, and you will receive, that your joy may be full."

John 14:6 Jesus said to him, "I am the way, the truth, and the life. No one comes to the Father except through Me."

**Pray believing you will receive what you ask.**

Mark 11:24-26 Jesus said, "Therefore I say to you, whatever things you ask when you pray, believe that you receive them, and you will have them."

**Pray in the Spirit.**

Ephesians 6:18 "Pray always with all prayer and supplication in the Spirit."

**Pray with the Holy Spirit's help.**

Romans 8:26 "Likewise the Spirit also helps in our weaknesses. For we do not know what we should pray for as we ought, but the Spirit Himself makes intercession for us with groanings which cannot be uttered. Now He who searches the hearts knows what the mind of the Spirit is, because He makes intercession for the saints according to the will of God."

**Pray confessing your sins and with humility.**

II Chronicles 7:14 "If My people who are called by My name will humble themselves, and pray and seek My face, and turn from their wicked ways, then I will hear from heaven, and will forgive their sin and heal their land."

**Pray with your whole heart.**

Jeremiah 29:13 "And you will seek Me and find Me, when you search for Me with all your heart."

## Will your prayer be answered?

If we abide in Him and His words abide in us our prayers will be answered.

John 15:7 Jesus said, "If you abide in Me, and My words abide in you, you will ask what you desire, and it shall be done for you. By this My Father is glorified, that you bear much fruit; so you will be My disciples."

If we ask according to His will, he hears us, and we will have our petitions!

1 John 5:14-15 "Now this is the confidence that we have in Him, that if we ask anything according to His will, He hears us. And if we know that He hears us, whatever we ask, we know that we have the petitions that we have asked of Him."

If we keep his commandments, love God and our fellowman, whatever we ask we shall receive.

1 John 3:22-23 "And whatever we ask we receive from Him, because we keep His commandments and do those things that are pleasing in His sight. And this is His commandment: that we should believe on the name of His Son Jesus Christ and love one another, as He gave us commandment."

## Does God anticipate the needs of His children?

He knows before we even ask.

Isaiah 65:24 "It shall come to pass that before they call, I will answer, and while they are still speaking, I will hear."

## Is there a limit to God's ability to help?

He can and will do exceedingly more than we can ask or think!

Ephesians 3:20 "Now to Him who is able to do exceedingly abundantly above all that we ask or think, according to the power that works in us, to Him be glory in the church by Christ Jesus to all generations, forever and ever. Amen."

## Under what condition does the Lord not hear prayer?

**God does not hear the prayer of an unrepentant sinner.**

John 9:31 "Now we know that God does not hear sinners; but if anyone is a worshipper of God and does His will, He hears him."

**If I enjoy a secret sin in my heart, the Lord will not hear.**

Psalms 66:18 "If I regard iniquity in my heart, the Lord will not hear."

**He certainly can not answer unless we ask, and sometimes we desire answers to satisfy our own lusts.**

James 4:3 "Yet you do not have because you do not ask. You ask and do not receive, because you ask amiss, that you may spend it on your pleasures."

**We must be obedient for our prayers to be answered.**

Proverbs 28:9 "One who turns away his ear from hearing the law, even his prayer is an abomination."

## What is meditation?

Meditation means to become absorbed in thought or consider something quietly, soberly, and deeply. It also means to reflect, wonder or marvel on something that has been said or read.

1 Timothy 4:15 "Let no one despise your youth, but be an example to the believers in word, in conduct, in love, in spirit, in faith, in purity. Till I come, give attention to reading, to exhortation, to doctrine. Do not neglect the gift that is in you, which was given to you by prophecy with the laying on of the hands of the eldership. Meditate on these things; give yourself entirely to them, that your progress may be evident to all. Take heed to yourself and to the doctrine. Continue in them, for in doing this you will save both yourself and those who hear you."

# When are we to meditate?

**We are to meditate and teach our children when we sit in our house, when we walk by the wayside, when we lie down and when we rise up.**

> Deuteronomy 11:18-21 "Therefore you shall lay up these words of mine in your heart and in your soul, and bind them as a sign on your hand, and they shall be as frontlets between your eyes. You shall teach them to your children, speaking of them when you sit in your house, when you walk by the way, when you lie down, and when you rise up. And you shall write them on the doorposts of your house and on your gates, that your days and the days of your children may be multiplied in the land of which the Lord swore to your fathers to give them, like the days of the heavens above the earth."

### The Bible exhorts us to meditate day and night.

> Psalms 1:1-2 "Blessed is the man who walks not in the counsel of the ungodly, nor stands in the path of sinners, nor sits in the seat of the scornful; but his delight is in the law of the Lord, and in His law he mediates day and night."

### We are to meditate on our beds.

> Psalms 63:6 "When I remember You on my bed, I meditate on You in the night watches."

I trust I have shown you prayer is simply a means we use to approach God, our heavenly Father, in word, or thought, to give thanks, praise, or to worship; it means to make an entreaty, petition or an earnest request on behalf of ourselves or someone else. It is simply talking to your heavenly Father as you would your earthly Father.

Jesus modeled the Lord's Prayer for us, showing us a good way to direct our prayers. I hope I have shown the importance of praying, that we are to pray at all times in the name of Jesus, the conditions for answered prayers, and the reasons for unanswered prayers.

We are to meditate, think, or reflect on what the Word of God says. As we do, we gain great insight into the Word of God. When we pray, it allows us to see what a mighty God we serve. It builds our faith, and when we are faced with a spiritual battle, we always have our shield of faith ready to defend us!! The following is awesome and so true!

I asked for strength that I might achieve;
I was made weak that I might learn to obey.
I asked for health that I might do greater things.
I was given infirmity that I might do better things.
I asked for riches that I might be happy;
I was given poverty that I might be wise.
I asked for power that I might have the praise of men
I was given weakness that I might feel the need of God.
I asked for all things that I might enjoy life;
I was given life that I might enjoy all things.
I received nothing that I asked for but all I hoped for;
I am among men most blessed. In spite of myself
My prayers were answered!

Author Unknown

# Chapter 13

## HOW DO I WALK IN LOVE

God has called us to a higher level of living. God says he wants our behavior to change now that we have become new creatures in Christ. Regardless of what great and mighty accomplishments we might perform, if we do not love, our works are not acceptable to God. His Word teaches us the greatest commandment is to love the Lord our God with all our heart, with all our soul and with all our mind. The second great commandment is like it; we must love our neighbor as ourselves.

We are told to love one another for love is of God and everyone who loves is born of God and knows God. He who does not love does not know God, for God is love.[104] Until people are born of God, they cannot love properly, because they do not have God in their lives. When we like what someone does for us or how they make us feel, our "love" is built on selfishness. It's what others do for us that cause us to think we love them. There are many people who commit suicide and/or murder in the name of "love," because in their selfishness, they believe the person on which they have set their affections is the only one who can meet their needs. It is all about them, their needs and demands.

I have often jokingly said that God instituted marriage so we could learn how to love. The longer I live, the more I believe this is actually true. Ultimately, loving someone is often denying your self, so the other person can do what they desire. We must die daily to our old man and our old selfish ways of doing things. No longer looking out for me, me, me and I, I, I. We are to become like Jesus, who committed the greatest act of selflessness when He died on the cross for our sins. He denied Himself and was willing to suffer and be crucified so that we could be forgiven of our sins and spend eternity in heaven. Now we are to be willing to die to our own selfish desires.

In most marriages, after we have been married for a while the devil often convinces us that our partner doesn't love us very much. Because our enemy, the devil, plants ugly thoughts in our minds, at times we see our mates as selfish and uncaring. This is one reason there are so many divorces. Satan doesn't have any new tactics. What he is doing in marriages today, he has done thousands of times before and he will continue to do until the end of time. I remember thinking these same negative thoughts about my husband and talking to the Lord about them. The Lord spoke to me and said, "Your husband loves you as much as he is capable of loving anyone, now you teach him to love!" Wow, what a tall order! Then the realization struck me that I did not know how to teach him to love, because I did not know how myself. I feel sure my husband thought that I was selfish and unloving at times. When I told the Lord how unloving my husband could be, His response was in the form of a question. He asked, "When are you the most unlovable?" My reply was that I was most unlovable when I needed love and understanding the most. What a revelation for me! That's when my husband needed love and understanding the most!

God has called us to love and to love not only the lovable but also the unlovable which is impossible to do in our own strength. It is only as we allow Him to love through us that we can accomplish what He has called us to do. With these thoughts in mind let's take a look at a new way of living—by loving.

## How important is love to a Christian?

The first and greatest commandment is to love God and the second commandment is to love our neighbor as we love ourselves.

### God speaks to us in the following scriptures about love.

Matthew 22:37-39 Jesus said to him, "You shall love the Lord your God with all your heart, with all your soul, and with all your mind. This is the first and great commandment. And the second is like it: You shall love your neighbor as yourself."

1 John 4:7-11 "Beloved, let us love one another, for love is of God; and everyone who loves is born of God and knows God. He who does not love does not know God, for God is love. In this the love of God was manifested toward us, that God has sent His only begotten Son into the world, that we might live through Him. In this is love,

117

not that we loved God, but that He loved us and sent His Son to be the propitiation for our sins. Beloved, if God so loved us, we also ought to love one another." God demonstrated how much He loved us by sending His son to die for our sins so that we can have eternal life. When we have been born again, the love of God enters our hearts and we are to show that love to the world.

1 John 2:15-16 "Do not love the world or the things in the world. If anyone loves the world, the love of the Father is not in him. All that is in the world—the lust of the flesh, the lust of the eyes, and the pride of life—is not of the Father but is of the world." This means that we are not to give priority to the things of this world in an effort to satisfy our flesh (the things we "think" will make us happy).

1 John 3:14-23 "We know that we have passed from death to life, because we love the brethren. He who does not love his brother abides in death. Whoever hates his brother is a murderer, and you know that no murderer has eternal life abiding in him. By this we know love, because He laid down His life for us. And we also ought to lay down our lives for the brethren. But whoever has this world's goods, and sees his brother in need, and shuts up his heart from him, how does the love of God abide in him? My little children let us not love in word or in tongue, but in deed and in truth. And by this we know that we are of the truth, and shall assure our hearts before Him. If our heart condemns us, God is greater than our heart, and knows all things. Beloved, if our heart does not condemn us, we have confidence toward God. Whatever we ask we receive from Him, because we keep His commandments and do those things that are pleasing in His sight. And this is His commandment: that we should believe on the name of His Son Jesus Christ and love one another, as He gave us commandment."

1 John 4:12-21 "No one has seen God at any time. If we love one another, God abides in us, and His love has been perfected in us. By this we know that we abide in Him, and He in us, because He has given us of His Spirit. And we have seen and testify that the Father has sent the Son as Savior of the world. Whoever confesses that Jesus is the Son of God, God abides in him, and he in God. And we have known and believed the love that God has for us. God is love, and he who abides in love abides in God and God in him. Love has been perfected among us in this: that we may have boldness in the Day of Judgment; because as He is, so are we in this world. There is no fear

in love; but perfect love casts out fear, because fear involves torment. But he who fears has not been made perfect in love. We love Him because He first loved us. If someone says, "I love God," and hates his brother, he is a liar; for he who does not love his brother whom he has seen, how can he love God whom he has not seen? And this commandment we have from Him: that he who loves God must love his brother also."

These scriptures tell us we are to judge ourselves—our behavior, our attitude, and our motives. It is our responsibility to check our hearts. No one else can, but we know whether or not we love and there is a remedy! That's the good news!

1 Peter 4:7-11 "But the end of all things is at hand; therefore be serious and watchful in your prayers." And above all things have fervent love for one another, for "love will cover a multitude of sins." Be hospitable to one another without grumbling. As each one has received a gift, minister it to one another, as good stewards of the manifold grace of God. If anyone speaks, let him speak as the oracles of God. If anyone ministers, let him do it as with the ability which God supplies, that in all things God may be glorified through Jesus Christ, to whom belong the glory and the dominion forever and ever. Amen.

Isn't the phrase "love will cover a multitude of sins" one of the most comforting scriptures when we have done something we should not have done to God or to man, or when someone has sinned against us? God's love forgives us when we repent. Our love for others will not cause God to pass up or pardon their sins, but it will enable us to pass up the faults of others and not hold grudges ourselves.

All these scriptures clearly show us, the commandment to love is imperative in our Christian Walk.

## What is love?

### There are three different kinds of love: Eros, phileo, and agape.

Eros refers to romantic love. This is a strong feeling that is almost uncontrollable. Eros love is experienced by non-Christians as well as by Christians. It involves an attraction that draws you to another person. They make you feel "good" about yourself. Your heart beats faster when you see them. You become nervous. Your hands become sweaty. As you get to know them better, you want to spend all your time with them. If a couple has Eros without the accompanying phileo or agape love, then nothing is left when the Eros fades—nothing but emptiness, frustration, and perhaps even a lack of motivation to continue in the marriage relationship.

Phileo refers to brotherly love which means to be fond of someone. Phileo love is experienced by non-Christians as well as Christians. Sometimes you feel this kind of love for a person because they make you feel good about yourself. It could also be based on admiration or appreciation for what they do for you or others.

Eros and phileo are selfish types of love, because they are based on how they make you feel. To endure, these types of love have to continue to make you feel good. If you only possess Eros love, it will fade when the feeling fades. If you only have phileo love for another person, that love will be replaced by disdain and a lack of respect when he makes a mistake or falls from the pedestal on which you have placed him.

Agape refers to God's kind of love which is giving and unselfish. It is not based on feelings and causes you to think of the other person before you think of yourself. Agape love is unconditional and is given whether the person has "earned" it or not. It's the kind of love that is forgiving for wrongs suffered. It picks up those who fall and stumble. Only God's grace can help us achieve this kind of love. It was demonstrated in its fullness when Jesus gave His life for ours before we ever did anything for him.

## What are the rewards of expressing love?

Galatians 6:7 "Do not be deceived, God is not mocked; for whatever a man sows, that he will also reap." If we sow acts of kindness by giving and doing for others, what will we reap? According to scripture, if we sow love, we will reap love! Whatever you want in your life, you have to sow that kind of seed. If you want love, sow love seeds. If you want forgiveness, sow forgiveness seeds. If you want understanding, sow understanding seeds etc. We receive back into our lives what we sow into the lives of others.

## How do we express love?

1 Corinthians 13 "Though I speak with the tongues of men and of angels, but have not love, I have become sounding brass or a clanging cymbal. And though I have the gift of prophecy, and understand all mysteries and all knowledge, and though I have all faith, so that I could remove mountains, but have not love, I am nothing. And though I bestow all my goods to feed the poor, and though I give my body to be burned, but have not love, it profits me nothing."

If I speak in the tongues of men and even of angels, but have not love (that reasoning, intentional, spiritual devotion such as inspired by God's love for and in us) I am only a noisy gong or a clanging cymbal. And if I have prophetic powers—(that is, the gift of interpreting the divine will) and if I can remove mountains but have not love (God's love in me) I am nothing—a useless nobody. Even if I dole out all that I have to the poor in providing food, and if I surrender my body to be burned, but have not love (God's love in me) I gain nothing.

The foretelling of prophecy, which is the prediction of events far in the future, is perhaps the greatest proof of the divine inspiration of the Scriptures. In relating this to the importance of love, Paul said that if someone understood all prophecies and all mysteries, and if he did not have love, it would profit nothing. Your greatest act means nothing if it is not motivated by love.

Paul tells of a man who gave all his goods to feed the poor, and was even willing to suffer martyrdom. Certainly, he who gives his life for the gospel stands high on the list of Christ's disciples. When the enemies of the gospel stoned Stephen to death, he saw a vision of Christ standing at the right hand of God, as if to welcome him home. Stephen had such love for his enemies that, in Acts 7:60, "He knelt down and cried out with a loud voice, 'Lord, do not charge them with this sin.' And when he had said this, he fell asleep." Evidently his prayers were answered. Saul, the ringleader of the group who killed Stephen, saw the love of Jesus in action and was later converted to Christ. Saul, whose name was later changed to Paul, became the champion of the Christian faith.

Even martyrdom without love is not enough. A Muslim will endure great hardships, incur personal danger, and will give his life for the cause in which he believes. Why does he do that? It is not because of love. While there may be mixed motives, it is generally because of his hatred for the infidels and the rewards he hopes to gain. He may die for his cause, but the motive that inspires him is not love, but his own sadly warped self-interest.

## So . . . How do we love?

Love suffers long and is kind; love does not envy; love does not parade itself, is not puffed up, does not behave rudely, does not seek its own, is not provoked, thinks no evil; does not rejoice in iniquity, but rejoices in the truth; bears all things, believes all things, hopes all things, and endures all things. After Paul shows us how important love is in the life of a Christian, he goes on to speak about what love really means.

## Love suffers long.

Love bears up under anything and everything that comes its way. It is ever ready to believe the best of every person. Love endures under all circumstances and does it without weakening. Love gives a person the power to be patient when things go wrong as well as the power to remain calm when others lose their "cool". There are people who have exceptional talents and abilities, but when an unexpected situation arises, they panic and "blow their top". Love does not act this way. Love is long-suffering.

## Love is patient.

Love understands the limitations and weaknesses of humanity. Love hopes for the best to be revealed in every person. A mother's love is an example of this quality. If her child does wrong, and all others give up faith in him, a loving mother will keep on praying and believing for the best for her child in that situation. Patience is a quality of Divine love.

## Love is kindness in action.

Love is kind to all and will not purposely hurt others. Love gets no pleasure in making life more difficult for people. Kind, loving actions will point men to the Christ you serve. Always remember—**you represent Christ**. Let your actions cause others to see Christ in you and want to be like you. In Ephesians God says "Therefore be imitators of God as dear children. And walk in love, as Christ also has loved us and given Himself for us."[105]

## Love is not jealous.

In today's world, many people seem concerned only with themselves. It is easy to become envious of what others can do and what they have, but this is not God's way. When blessings come to our neighbors, friends, and families, we should not have envy in our hearts. Love will be glad and rejoice with others in their good fortune.

Another growing tendency these days is that some people fight for success. Even Christians are in danger of doing this. Some wish to be the greatest preacher, the finest singer, or want to be looked upon as the most important leader in the church. Often Christians are not genuinely happy to see God moving in the lives of others or in other denominations or groups. The love of Christ is not jealous of the blessings of others but desires for success to come to all.

"Let love be without hypocrisy. Abhor what is evil. Cling to what is good. Be kindly affectionate to one another with brotherly love, in honor giving preference to one another; not lagging in diligence, fervent in spirit, serving the Lord; rejoicing in hope, patient in tribulation, continuing steadfastly in prayer; distributing to the needs of the saints, given to hospitality."[106]

## Love is humble, not conceited or proud.

Often when people become successful and gain influence, they become insufferable. Their drive for power can cause them to become contemptuous of the rights of others. They forget that others helped them to become successful, and they also forget that without God, they are nothing. Pride can destroy all that is good and decent in people. The scriptures tell us we should not elevate ourselves because every one who exalts himself will be humbled . . . and he who humbles himself will be exalted. The cure for unholy ambition is humility and Divine love.

## Love is courteous not ill-mannered.

Love reveals itself by our behavior. Sometimes people act so kind while in public, but then behave like tyrants when at home. True courtesy should be an aspect of all of our relationships. Ask yourself these questions: Am I treating all the people in my life the way I want to be treated? Am I as courteous to them as I want them to be to me? Remember that love is courteous to everyone at all times.

## Love is not selfish and does not demand its own way.

Undoubtedly the largest arena where love, or the lack of it, is played out is in the context of marriage. One of the biggest obstacles married couples have to overcome is selfishness. Each person wants his own way. Often one partner wants to control the actions of the other. Other times one partner is jealous of the other.

"Wives, submit to your own husbands, as to the Lord. For the husband is head of the wife, as also Christ is head of the church; and He is the Savior of the body. Therefore, just as the church is subject to Christ, so let the wives be to their own husbands in everything. Husbands, love your wives, just as Christ also loved the church and gave Himself for her, that He might sanctify and cleanse her with the washing of water by the word, that He might present her to Himself a glorious church, not having spot or wrinkle or any such thing, but that she should be holy and without blemish. So husbands ought to love their own wives as their own bodies; he who loves his wife loves himself. For no one ever hated his own flesh, but nourishes and cherishes it, just as the Lord does the church."[107]

When a wife is submissive to her husband, she is not ruled by selfishness. She does not demand her own way but always considers her husband's desires and feelings. We know that Christ loved us so much that He gave His own life for us. If a husband loves his wife as Christ loved us, then he will not be self-centered and insist on having his own way. His actions will always be guided by what is best for his wife and for the family. If two people seek the other person's best interest above their own, they will have a peaceful home. Marriage brings two people into a relationship where the two become "one"; therefore, when one partner is blessed, those same blessings come to the other partner. There is no need for competition or jealousy, because the blessings and accomplishments of one also belong to the other. Partners should rejoice with each other over the successes that come their way.

The greatest gift that God will ever give you is a companion—someone with whom you can share your life—someone who will love you with all your short-comings—someone who will be there in sickness and health—and someone who cares for you whether you are rich or poor. We must make it our top priority to treat this most valuable gift of God with great love and respect.

## Love is not irritable and does not have a quick temper.

One who has Divine love will not be easily irritated. Some professing Christians are given to a fearfully quick temper. They are terribly sensitive and cannot bear to have the least thing cross them. They excuse themselves by saying their mom or dad had a fiery temper. Our heavenly Father does not act this way and we need to pattern ourselves after Him.

## Love does not keep a record of wrongs.

Love pays no attention to a suffered wrong. Love thinks no evil. It is sad that some people live in a state of constant suspicion. If someone does wrong to you, you must be ready to forgive that person and forget that wrong just as Christ has forgiven you. We are to forgive someone who sins against us seventy times seven.

## Love is not happy with evil—but rejoices with truth.

Some people are very happy when they hear a bad report about others. In fact, they may even feel elated when someone falls by the wayside, believing that somehow they will profit by that person's failure. True Christian love, however, rejoices not in evil but in goodness and truth. "Love never fails. But whether there are prophecies, they will fail; whether there are tongues, they will cease; whether there is knowledge, it will vanish away. For we know in part and we prophesy in part. But when that which is perfect has come, then that which is in part will be done away. When I was a child, I spoke as a child, I understood as a child, I thought as a child; but when I became a man, I put away childish things. For now we see in a mirror, dimly, but then face to face. Now I know in part, but then I shall know just as I also am known. And now abides faith, hope, love, these three; but the greatest of these is love."[108]

In 1974, I was taught that love is a choice, not a feeling. I determined if love was a choice, I would choose to love. When we make a choice to love, God through His matchless grace gives us the ability. We can not love others the way God wants us to love them through our own efforts. It is only through the power of the Holy Spirit that we are able to truly love anyone, especially the unlovable. We must choose to love.

What greater gift can we give someone or have someone give us than to truly love them with the kind of love that only comes from God? His unconditional love means accepting others and loving them just as they are. As we love others with agape love, not only will they be transformed by that love, but we will be changed as well.

# Chapter 14

## HOW DO YOU WALK IN THE SPIRIT?

W alk in the Spirit, and you shall not fulfill the lust of the flesh. For the flesh lusts against the Spirit and the Spirit against the flesh; and these are contrary to one another, so that you do not do the things you wish.[109] Many times Christians have a general understanding of terms used either by other Christians or in the Bible, but they don't grasp the actual meaning. What is walking in the Spirit? When the Bible speaks of a person's "walk," it simply means the way he lives his life. Our walk refers to our demeanor, our conduct, or even the way we are perceived by others. These are all components of our "walk."

Now we know what our walk consists of, but how do we walk in the spirit? It is rather like when I was learning to paint. When I read about painting the negative space I didn't understand what it meant. How do I do that? I know what negative means and I know what space means, but how do I paint something that isn't there? I finally had to ask someone what it meant. It is really very simple—it is painting the background of a picture that is not an object! Walking in the Spirit is also very simple; it can be summed up in two words: trust and obey. The words may be simple, but trusting God and His Word (The Holy Bible) and obeying what the Word says is not easy.

When a person is first introduced to the idea of walking in the spirit, he must ask himself how this is done. He learns to walk in the spirit just as a baby learns to walk in the natural. When a baby sees others walking, he tries to walk, falls down, holds out his hands to the parent, gets up, and tries it again and again until he masters the art of walking. It has been shown in the last chapter that when a person is born again, he is no longer under Satan's power unless he allows it. Before salvation man was ruled by Satan, his own selfishness, the lust of the flesh, the lust of the eye, and the pride of life. We also realized that the root of all sin is selfishness. Everything revolves around me, me, me, I, I, I. God says that is the way our old man behaved, but we are new creatures in Christ. He wants our behavior to change. We are to be transformed from the old man and the way he walked into a new creature that walks in a different way. We are to be transformed by the renewing of our minds. The Bible teaches us a new way of thinking that is completely opposite from the way we thought before we came to Christ. As our minds are renewed by the Word of God, our new spirit man wants to obey God; however, we have a battle on our hands. The old way of thinking rises up and tries to influence the new man. This is where our battle begins. Are we going to trust and obey God, or are we going to do what our flesh begs us to do? Until we get our "walking" legs, sometimes we stumble, but God picks us up and encourages us to try again. He doesn't condemn us any more than earthly parents condemn their babies when they are learning to walk. He is ever encouraging us to obey because He knows everything He asks us to do ultimately works for our good.

As we begin this walk in the spirit, the first thing we have to determine is that we want to walk in the spirit. We must be willing to be willing! We make the choice to walk in the Spirit and then God gives us His grace to do so. Why should we want to walk in the Spirit? First, it is commanded by God, "Take careful heed to do the commandment and the law which Moses the servant of the Lord commanded you, to love the Lord your God, to walk in all His ways, to keep His commandments, to hold fast to Him, and to serve Him will all your heart and with all your soul."[110] When Jesus was asked which was the greatest commandment He replied: "You shall love the Lord your God will all your heart, with all your soul, and with all your mind. This is the first and great commandment and the second is like it, "You shall love your neighbor as yourself." Everything that the law and the prophets told them they should do is summed up in these two commandments.[111] Jesus also tells us in His Word; "This thing commanded I them, saying, obey my voice, and I will be your God, and you will be my people. Walk in all the ways I have commanded you; that it may be well with you."[112] In Psalms 1:1-2 "A person is blessed who does not walk in the counsel of the ungodly, nor does he stand in the path of sinners, or in the seat of the scornful, but he delights in the law of the Lord, and on it he meditates day and night." God promises us rest for our souls if we walk in the old paths where the good way is found.

But there is more. We were buried with Him through our baptism into death. Just as Christ was raised from the dead by the glory of the

Father, even so we should also walk in newness of life.[113] When a person is being baptized; I like to envision him being immersed as the "old man" being put to death, and when he comes forth from the baptismal pool, as being the new creature. "If you are raised with Christ, you are to seek those things which are above, where Christ is sitting at the right hand of God. Therefore, set your mind on things above, not on things on the earth. For you died and your life is hidden with Christ in God. Therefore we must put to death the things that identify us with the old man. Do not lie to one another because we have put off the old man with his deeds, and have put on the new man who is renewed in knowledge according to the image of Him who created us."[114] This new creature must be transformed by the renewing of his mind so that he may prove the good, acceptable and perfect will of God. His mind is transformed as he reads in God's Word what He wants him to do, and how He wants him to live.

We have been in the world, thought like the world, been under the influence of the world, and acted like the world. We are what the Bible calls the natural man, carnal man, or the man of flesh. Until we come to realize that the ways of the world only lead to death and destruction and by an act of our will decide we will no longer live that way, we will be carnal. We will no longer live as carnal beings when we repent of going our own way and exercising our own will. We must confess Jesus and His precious blood as the only way of salvation and receive Him as Lord and Master of our lives. To be carnally minded is death but to be spiritually minded is life and peace.

Those of us who are in Christ Jesus who do not walk according to the flesh but according to the Spirit are not condemned. If we walk in the Spirit, we will not fulfill the lust of the flesh. The flesh lusts against the Spirit, and the Spirit lusts against the flesh. They are contrary to one another, and we sometimes end up doing what we don't want to do.

I say then: "Walk in the Spirit, and you shall not fulfill the lust of the flesh, so that you do not do the things that you wish. But if you are led by the Spirit, you are not under the law. Now the works of the flesh are evident, which are: adultery, fornication, uncleanness, lewdness, idolatry, sorcery, hatred, contentions, jealousies, outbursts of wrath, selfish ambitions, dissensions, heresies, envy, murders, drunkenness, revelries, and the like; of which I tell you beforehand, just as I also told you in time past, that those who practice such things will not inherit the kingdom of God. But the fruit of the Spirit is love, joy, peace, longsuffering, kindness, goodness, faithfulness, gentleness, self-control. Against such there is no law. And those who are Christ's have crucified the flesh with its passions and desires. If we live in the Spirit, let us also walk in the Spirit. Let us not become conceited, provoking one another, envying one another. Do not be deceived, God is not mocked; for whatever a man sows, that he will also reap. For he who sows to his flesh will of the flesh reap corruption, but he who sows to the Spirit will of the Spirit reap everlasting life. And let us not grow weary while doing good, for in due season we shall reap if we do not lose heart. Therefore, as we have opportunity, let us do good to all, especially to those who are of the household of faith."[115]

The temptations of life are the greatest stumbling blocks to our walking in the Spirit. All of us are tempted either by the lust of the flesh, the lust of the eye, or the pride of life. The underlying cause of all temptation is still selfishness. We want something we don't have. The lust of the flesh usually appeals to food, drink, sex, or emotional needs we want met. Also the flesh doesn't want to deal with the problems of life. The lust of the eye is something we see that we want. The pride of life has to do with positions, plaudits, or popularity we desire above others.

There are many ways of walking in the Spirit. One way is to change our thinking. As a man thinks in his heart so is he.[116] This is why it is so important to meditate on the things that are true, noble, just, pure, lovely, things of a good report, and things virtuous and praiseworthy. If we change our thinking, the peace of God will be with us.[117] David wrote in the Psalms, I will set nothing wicked before my eyes. He knew that if he saw something wicked he might be enticed by what he saw.

He knew that each one is tempted when he is drawn away and enticed by his own desires. When desire conceives, it gives birth to sin; and sin, when it is full-grown brings forth death.[118] Certainly David knew from first hand experience. He was married, but one evening as he was walking on his roof top, he saw a beautiful woman as she was taking her bath. He was enticed by her beauty, and he desired to have her. He acted on his temptation and had her brought to him. Later when Bathsheba told him she was with child, he connived in his heart and devised a plan to have her husband Uriah murdered to hide his sin of adultery.

We are admonished in many, many scriptures to walk in love, as Christ has loved us and has given Himself for us.[119] If we walk in the light as He is in the light we have fellowship with one another, and the blood of Jesus Christ cleanses us from all sin.[120] Just as you have received Christ

Jesus the Lord, so walk in Him, rooted and built up and established in the faith, as you have been taught, abounding in it with thanksgiving.

When Paul heard of someone's salvation he did not cease to pray for them and to ask that they would be filled with the knowledge of God's will in all wisdom and spiritual understanding, that they might walk worthy of the Lord, fully pleasing Him, being fruitful in every good work and increasing in the knowledge of God.[121]

The longer I live the more I am convinced that we cannot experience or enjoy the fruit of the spirit unless we walk in the Spirit. If we want the fruit of the Spirit which is love, joy, peace, longsuffering, kindness, goodness, faithfulness, gentleness, and self-control to become a reality in our life, we must walk in the Spirit. We must repent of the sins we commit in the flesh and ask God to forgive us. He then cleanses us and forgives us from all unrighteousness.[122] We make the choice to walk in the Spirit, and He gives us the grace to do so.

I am not talking about a wish, or even what we purpose to do, but our deliberate choice. The will is the deciding power to which all that is in man must yield obedience. If we are to walk in the Spirit, God must take possession of us in our will. It must be into this central will or personality that He enters. If God is reigning there by the power of His Spirit, all the rest of our nature must come under His sway; as the will is, so is the man. Regardless of how much our flesh clamors to have its way, the will always will rule over the flesh. Since a man's will is really the man's self, of course, what his will wants to do determines his actions. When we choose to do God's will and surrender our will to Him, we have done all we can do. God then begins to work in us to will and to do His good pleasure.

I have found the most beneficial thing to walking in the Spirit is to make a written declaration to God that I have surrendered my will to His Lordship. When you do this, it should be dated and kept where you see it daily. Then when the flesh rises up to entice you, or your emotions flare up to entrap you and pride wants to parade itself, you remind yourself you are going to do God's will.

When you first become a Christian, you might find it easy to obey the leading of the Lord when He says, "This is the way, walk ye in it." But there will come a time when temptation comes in an area where you are weakest, when it will be so easy to listen to the voice of "reason," especially when it tells you what you want to hear. Having already set your will to do God's will, regardless of the battle that ensues, you will find out you can not go against your convictions. What a glorious day that will be!!

As we keep the commandment to walk in His ways, which is obeying His Word, He becomes our God and we become His people. Then it will go well with us, we will be blessed, and we will find peace for our souls.

# Chapter 15

## HOW DO I WALK IN FAITH?

"Fear knocked on the door; Faith answered and no one was there." Faith is a growing thing. The longer we live and walk in the Spirit, the more our faith should grow. Before we came to Jesus Christ for salvation, we based all of our decisions on our soulish nature, (the man of flesh, or the carnal man who was under the dominion of Satan), and we relied on what we could hear, see, taste, touch, and smell. Now God is saying we must walk by faith and not by sight.[123]

**What is faith or trust?**

Strong's concordance states faith is conviction of religious truth, or the truthfulness of God, assurance, belief, faith, or knowing something is reliable. Webster's dictionary says faith is belief and trust in the loyalty of God; a firm belief in something for which there is no proof. Strong's concordance says trust is to anticipate with pleasure; expectation or confidence, faith, hope. Webster's Dictionary says trust is assured reliance on the character, ability, strength, or truth of someone or something. Trust is dependent on something in the future but built on past experiences.

Hebrews Chapter 11 is called the Hall of Faith because of all the people who believed God, and it was accounted to them for righteousness. They are wonderful examples of people who had faith in Biblical times, but today I want to make faith personal and applicable. The Bible says: Hebrews 11:1-2 "Now faith is the <u>substance</u> of things <u>hoped</u> for, the <u>evidence</u> of <u>things not seen</u>. For by it the elders obtained a good testimony."

What I am going to share with you is my personal interpretation of faith. Let me explain faith as I understand it. Faith is believing what the Bible says and acting upon it. As I stated before, faith is a growing thing. I believe hope always comes before faith. If faith is the substance of things for which we <u>hoped</u>, we must have hoped God would provide something for us; and we must have received it as something we could distinguish since substance is made up of matter and form. Also if faith is the evidence of things not seen, it must be something similar to the wind. We cannot see the wind, but we can see the effects of the wind if it is blowing. We all know that we have sinned. Someone tells us the good news of God's Word. Jesus came into the world to save sinners. We are told that we can be forgiven of all our sins because Jesus died on the cross to pay for our sins. We hope it is true, we follow the steps laid out in the Bible of repenting of our sins, and we confess Jesus as Lord of our lives. Then we are baptized believing we will be born again. Many times there is a peace that permeates our being, which is the evidence that what we were told was true; so our faith grows.

Sometimes if we are too young, we are not conscious of any immediate change; but over time the things we used to do no longer interest us and we know we have been changed. We know the seed of faith has been planted. Then we learn to pray and God answers our prayers, and that seed sends out roots. Then we read God's Word and find out His promises are true. The root produces a tree. Then we become like David when he slew the giant, Goliath. He knew God had been with him when he killed the lion and the bear, and he trusted God would be with him when he met Goliath. God did not let him down, and David became a great man of faith. As we read God's Word, act upon it, and find out it is true, we become great men and women of faith.

When we walk in faith, we believe the Word of God is true before we see physical results. What we see, hear, taste, touch, and smell may contradict what God's Word tells us to do and cause our emotions to rebel. We may have to humble ourselves and swallow our pride to do what His Word says; however, we do what His Word tells us to do because we believe God's Word is true and He can be trusted to keep His Word.

None of us ever come to God initially with all the faith we will ever have. It is as we obey and see the results of obedience that we begin to trust Him. As we trust Him our faith grows. It is ever increasing! Results bring more obedience, which brings more faith. When David killed the lion, he <u>hoped</u> God would be with him; and God was with him. His faith grew so that when he met the bear, he <u>believed</u> God would be with him; and he slew the bear. When he faced Goliath, David <u>had the faith</u> God would be with him; and of course, He was. Can you see how David's faith grew? I believe our faith works in the same fashion.

## The first step of faith is saving faith.

**Hebrews 11:6** says "Without faith it is impossible to please Him, for he who comes to God must believe that He is, and that He rewards those who diligently seek Him." The Bible says everyone knows there is a God. Some people will not admit it because they do not want to change their evil ways.

**Romans 12:3** "I say, through the grace given to me, to everyone who is among you, not to think of himself more highly than he ought to think, but to think soberly, as God has dealt to each one a measure of faith." Everyone has been given enough faith to believe there is a God.

**Romans 10:14-17** "How then shall they call on Him in whom they have not believed? And how shall they believe in Him of whom they have not heard? And how shall they hear without a preacher? And how shall they preach unless they are sent? As it is written: "How beautiful are the feet of those who preach the gospel of peace, who bring glad tidings of good things!" But they have not all obeyed the gospel. Isaiah says, "Lord, who has believed our report?" So then faith comes by hearing, and hearing by the word of God." These verses show the importance of having someone preach the Gospel to the unlearned. Our faith grows as we hear the Word of God proclaimed and then act on what we hear.

**Ephesians 2:8** "By grace you have been saved through faith, and that not of yourselves; it is the gift of God, not of works, lest anyone should boast." God saves us when we believe in His Word. It's not that which we do, if it were, we would be proud and boastful of our ability.

**Galatians 3:2** "This only I want to learn from you: Did you receive the Spirit by the works of the law, or by the hearing of faith? Are you so foolish? Having begun in the Spirit, are you now being made perfect by the flesh?" This reiterates that it is not living by the law and striving in our own humanity but simply believing.

**Galatians 3:11** "That no one is justified by the law in the sight of God is evident, for 'the just shall live by faith.'"

## How important is faith to a new Christian?

**1 Corinthians 15:12-17** "If Christ is preached that He has been raised from the dead, how do some among you say that there is no resurrection of the dead? If there is no resurrection of the dead, then Christ has not risen. And if Christ is not risen, then our preaching is empty and your faith is also empty. Yes, and we are found false witnesses of God, because we have testified of God that He raised up Christ, whom He did not raise up—if in fact the dead do not rise. For if the dead do not rise, and then Christ is not risen. And if Christ is not risen, your faith is futile; you are still in your sins!" If we are not taught to live by faith and believe, we are without hope in this world!

**Romans 5:1-2** "Therefore, having been justified by faith, we have peace with God through our Lord Jesus Christ, through whom also we have access by faith into this grace in which we stand, and rejoice in hope of the glory of God." We have been justified by our faith. This means it is as though we had never sinned and that our sins are forgiven forever, as far as the East is from the West. We have peace with God, and we have access to His grace.

**James 1:6-8** "If any of you lacks wisdom, let him ask of God, who gives to all liberally and without reproach, and it will be given to him. But let him ask in faith, with no doubting, for he who doubts is like a wave of the sea driven and tossed by the wind. For let not that man suppose that he will receive anything from the Lord; he is a double-minded man, unstable in all his ways." Without faith we will not receive anything from the Lord; we are double-minded and unstable in all our ways.

## Is faith for salvation all we ever receive?

**2 Thessalonians 1:3** "We are bound to thank God always for you, brethren, as it is fitting, because your faith grows exceedingly, and the love of every one of you all abounds toward each other." This says our faith grows!

**Romans 1: 16-17** "I am not ashamed of the gospel of Christ, for it is the power of God to salvation for everyone who believes, for the Jew first and also for the Greek. For in it the righteousness of God is revealed from faith to faith; as it is written, 'The just shall live by faith.'" According to these verses our faith grows from faith to faith, and we are to live and walk in faith in the Word of God.

## Do Christians have different levels of faith?

**1 Corinthians 12:7-9** "But the manifestation of the Spirit is given to each one for the profit of all: for to one is given the word of wisdom through the Spirit, to another the word of knowledge through the same Spirit, to another faith by the same Spirit, to another, gifts of healings by the same Spirit." Some have the gift of faith, which is a special gift of the Holy Spirit for a special occasion.

**Galatians 5:22** "The fruit of the Spirit is love, joy, peace, longsuffering, kindness, goodness, faithfulness, gentleness, self-control. Against such there is no law." Faith in God and obeying His Word produces over time the fruit of the Spirit.

**Romans 4:16-23** "Therefore it is of faith that it might be according to grace, so that the promise might be sure to all the seed, not only to those who are of the law, but also to those who are of the faith of Abraham, who is the father of us all (as it is written, 'I have made you a father of many nations') in the presence of Him whom he believed God, who gives life to the dead and calls those things which do not exist as though they did; who, contrary to hope, in hope believed, so that he became the father of many nations, according to what was spoken, 'So shall your descendants be.' And not being weak in faith, he did not consider his own body, already dead (since he was about a hundred years old), and the deadness of Sarah's womb. He did not waver at the promise of God through unbelief, but was strengthened in faith, giving glory to God, and being fully convinced that what He had promised He was also able to perform. And therefore it was accounted to him for righteousness. Now it was not written for his sake alone that it was imputed to him, but also for us. It shall be imputed to us who believe in Him who raised up Jesus our Lord from the dead, who was delivered up because of our offenses, and was raised because of our justification." Abraham was the grandfather of faith. He had strong faith, not weak faith, implying that there are those with weak faith.

**2 Corinthians 10:15** "Boasting not of things beyond measure, that is, in other men's labors, but having hope, that as your faith is increased, we shall be greatly enlarged by you in our sphere." Faith can and should be increased.

## The second step of faith is walking faith.

**2 Corinthians 5:**7 "We walk by faith, not by sight." What does this mean to you? How do we walk by faith? How did you learn to walk as a baby? You kept falling, getting up, and walking again. To walk in faith, we do what the Word of God says is true and do not listen to what our five senses tell us to do. If we fail we ask for forgiveness, get up and try again.

**Acts 14:21** "And when they had preached the gospel to that city and made many disciples, they returned to Lystra, Iconium, and Antioch, strengthening the souls of the disciples, exhorting them to continue in the faith, and saying, 'We must through many tribulations enter the kingdom of God.'" Preaching and exhortation helps one continue in the faith.

**Colossians 1:23** "If indeed you continue in the faith, grounded and steadfast, and are not moved away from the hope of the gospel which you heard, which was preached to every creature under heaven." Daily Bible reading keeps you on the right path. Attending church and Bible studies helps us continue walking in the faith.

**1 Timothy 1:18** "This charge I commit to you, son Timothy, according to the prophecies previously made concerning you, that by them you may wage the good warfare, having faith and a good conscience, which some having rejected, concerning the faith have suffered shipwreck." We keep our faith from becoming shipwrecked as we wage warfare according to the Word of God.

**1 Timothy 4:1** "Now the Spirit expressly says that in latter times some will depart from the faith, giving heed to deceiving spirits and doctrines of demons." We must always be on guard against deceiving spirits and listen careful to the doctrines taught so we will not be led astray.

**1 Timothy 6:20-21** "O Timothy! Guard what was committed to your trust, avoiding the profane and idle babblings and contradictions of what is falsely called knowledge—by professing it some have strayed concerning the faith." We are warned to be careful in listening to so-called teachers and experts that contradict Scripture.

**Jude 1:3** "Beloved, while I was very diligent to write to you concerning our common salvation, I found it necessary to write to you exhorting you to contend earnestly for the faith which was once for all delivered to the saints. For certain men have crept in unnoticed, who long ago were marked out for this condemnation, ungodly men, who turn the grace of our God into lewdness and deny the only Lord God, and our Lord Jesus Christ." We are to contend earnestly for the faith because there are many anti-christs who call themselves men of God.

**James 1:2** "My brethren, count it all joy when you fall into various trials, knowing that the testing of your faith produces patience. But let patience have its perfect work, that you may be perfect and complete, lacking nothing." Our faith will be tested, but it will produce patience, which is another shoot off the root to anchor the tree better.

**James 2:5** "Listen, my beloved brethren: Has God not chosen the poor of this world to be rich in faith and heirs of the kingdom which He promised to those who love Him?" Some intellectuals say that belief in Jesus Christ is an opiate for the common man! Perhaps that is because the poor know every thing they have and all they have become is because God loves them so much.

**James 2:14-26** "What does it profit, my brethren, if someone says he has faith but does not have works? Can faith save him? If a brother or sister is naked and destitute of daily food, and one of you says to them, 'Depart in peace, be warmed and filled,' but you do not give them the things which are needed for the body, what does it profit? Thus also faith by itself, if it does not have works, is dead. But someone will say, 'You have faith, and I have works.' Show me your faith without your works, and I will show you my faith by my works. You believe that there is one God. You do well. Even the demons believe—and tremble! But do you want to know, O foolish man, that faith without works is dead? Was not Abraham our father justified by works when he offered Isaac his son on the altar? Do you see that faith was working together with his works, and by works faith was made perfect? And the Scripture was fulfilled which says, 'Abraham believed God, and it was accounted to him for righteousness.' And he was called the friend of God. You see then that a man is justified by works, and not by faith only. Likewise, was not Rahab the harlot also justified by works when she received the messengers and sent them out another way? The body without the spirit is dead, so faith without works is dead also." Because we have faith in God and what He has done for us, we do the works He has called us to do.

**1 Timothy 6:11** "But you, O man of God, flee these things and pursue righteousness, godliness, faith, love, patience, gentleness. Fight the good fight of faith, lay hold on eternal life, to which you were also called and have confessed the good confession in the presence of many witnesses." We are to pursue faith.

## The next step of faith is standing faith.

When we think of someone standing for what they believe, we think of them facing the scoffer or resisting him.

**Ephesians 6:10-16** "Finally, my brethren, be strong in the Lord and in the power of His might. Put on the whole armor of God; that you may be able to stand against the wiles of the devil. We do not wrestle against flesh and blood, but against principalities, against powers, against the rulers of the darkness of this age, against spiritual hosts of wickedness in the heavenly places. Therefore take up the whole armor of God; that you may be able to withstand in the evil day, and having done all, to stand. Stand therefore, having girded your waist with truth, having put on the breastplate of righteousness, and having shod your feet with the preparation of the gospel of peace; above all, taking the shield of faith with which you will be able to quench all the fiery darts of the wicked one." When you know what you believe and why you believe it, and that belief is based on the Word of God, you can deflect all the darts of the enemy.

**2 John 1:10** "If anyone comes to you and does not bring this doctrine, do not receive him into your house nor greet him; for he who greets him shares in his evil deeds." We must guard our faith.

**James 5:14-15** "Is anyone among you sick? Let him call for the elders of the church, and let them pray over him, anointing him with oil in the name of the Lord. And the prayer of faith will save the sick, and the Lord will raise him up. And if he has committed sins, he will be forgiven." The prayer of faith is a mighty force to save the sick and forgive sins!

**1 Peter 5:8-9** "Be sober, be vigilant; because your adversary the devil walks about like a roaring lion, seeking whom he may devour. Resist him, steadfast in the faith, knowing that the same sufferings are experienced by your brotherhood in the world." You cannot fight the devil without resisting him with steadfast faith.

**1 John 5:4** "Whatever is born of God overcomes the world. And this is the victory that has overcome the world—our faith." Our faith gives us victory over the cares of the world.

## Now we come to running faith.

**Hebrews 12:1-2** "Therefore we also, since we are surrounded by so great a cloud of witnesses, let us lay aside every weight, and the sin which so easily ensnares us, and let us run with endurance the race that is set before us, looking unto Jesus, the author and finisher of our faith." We are encouraged to run with endurance the race set before us—looking to Jesus the author and finisher of our faith! We are going to win! He finishes our faith!!

**Revelations 12:11** "They overcame him by the blood of the Lamb and by the word of their testimony." We run the race as we overcome the world, the flesh, and the devil. It will be a test of our endurance, but we must keep our eyes focused on Jesus who aids us on the journey

## Lastly we finish our race with winning faith.

**2 Timothy 4:7** "I have fought the good fight (of faith), I have finished the race, and I have kept the faith. Finally, there is laid up for me the crown of righteousness, which the Lord, the righteous Judge, will give to me on that Day, and not to me only but also to all who have loved His appearing."

If we fight the good fight of faith, there is laid up for us a crown of righteousness the Lord will give us on that Day!!

So we see that all men are given a measure of faith. We learn to walk by faith just like we learn to walk in the natural. A baby's confidence grows as he learns to take one step and then another. Our faith grows as we read God's promises and hope and pray they are true. When God's promises are fulfilled in our lives, we begin to walk in confidence. Soon we see our tottering steps have become a long stride. If we keep a journal of the many times God answers our prayers, when we get in a tight spot we can bring out our journal and say with assurance just as David did, "God has seen me thru this and this and this; I am confident He will do it again!' As our faith becomes unshakable, we can throw off the weights that so easily beset us and run the race set before us. On that day when we stand before Jesus, we can say as Paul said, "I have fought the good fight, I have finished the race, I have kept the faith."

Then we will hear our Savior say "Well done My good and faithful servant; you have been faithful over a few things, I will make you ruler over many things. Enter into the joy of your Lord!"

Doubt sees the Obstacle
Faith sees the way.
Doubt sees a long dark night
Faith sees the day.
Doubt dreads to take a step
Faith soars on high.
Doubt thunders: "Who believes?"
Faith answers: "I."

# Chapter 16

## "I" CAN HEAR FROM GOD?

One of the most difficult things for me to believe was that I could hear from God. Perhaps it was because I didn't know what to expect. Maybe I thought God would use a loud speaker and announce, "Now hear this!" "Now hear this!" I struggled for years, yet all the while knowing I had received much insight from Him. Sometimes I even questioned if I was one of His sheep, because I didn't realize He was speaking to me. Perhaps I measured my success in hearing from God by others. Or probably the real reason was because the devil found out he could torment me if I thought I couldn't hear from God. My personal break through came one day when the thought came into my mind, "Where do you think all your good thoughts originate?" When I actually thought about it, I knew I was incapable of the thoughts that came into my mind. Wow! I finally got "it"! I do hear from God!

The devil wants all of us to believe we are not spiritual enough to hear from God. He wants us to think we are not worthy for the King of all creation, who is so busy managing this vast universe, to bother with the personal lives of billions of people. Why should Almighty God take the time to stoop down and speak to "little ole' me."

A lot of us think we do not need to hear from God; we tend to believe He gave us a brain, and He expects us to use it. All of us have heard the unbiblical cliché, "God helps those who help themselves," so we go our own way doing our own thing without ever consulting our Father.

He (the devil) undermines anything and everything to make us believe we do not hear from God. Since we have not had a lot of teaching on hearing God's voice, we tend to agree with the devil and waste a lot of time not believing we hear from God. So today I want us to establish the fact that God speaks (or communicates might be a better word) to us, and that we can hear and we do need to hear from Him.

Jesus says His sheep hear His voice. It is interesting to note that we are considered sheep, and Jesus is the shepherd. It is sheep that hear His voice and not lambs. By the time a lamb has become mature enough to be a sheep he has been fed, watered, watched over, and has come to trust the shepherd in every instance. We mature and become changed by our walk with God, and we come to trust Him in all things.

In the Bible we read: "His sheep hear his voice; and he calls his own sheep by name and leads them out. And when he brings out his own sheep, he goes before them; and the sheep follow him, for they know his voice. Yet they will by no means follow a stranger, but will flee from him, for they do not know the voice of strangers."[124]

Do we believe God's word? If so, then we know He speaks to us because His Word tells us we are His sheep, and His sheep know His voice. We must believe and settle in our heart that "I do hear from God." By this time you should believe in your heart that He loved you so much He sent his Son to die so you could have eternal life. You believe in your heart that God's Word is true. Just as you believe in your heart that all these precious promises are true, you now believe by faith you hear from God. If we do this when trying and confusing times come we will focus on God, rather than the circumstances.

God communicates His guidance through His written Word, the Scriptures or the Bible; through the spoken word by a preacher or a teacher; a still small voice that speaks a thought in our mind that didn't originate with us; providential circumstances or opened and closed doors; or an inner conviction of the Holy Spirit and an inward peace.

Let's look at other scriptures that tell us how he speaks:

**These scriptures say He speaks through teachers, preachers and evangelists.**

Romans 10: 13 "For whosoever shall call upon the name of the Lord shall be saved. How then shall they call on him in whom they have not believed? And how shall they believe in him of whom they have not heard? And how shall they hear without a preacher?"

John 14:23-24 "If anyone loves Me, he will keep My word; and My Father will love him, and We will come to him and make Our home with him. He who does not love Me does not keep My words;

and the word which you hear is not Mine but the Father's who sent Me."

**He speaks through the Holy Spirit** who now lives within us; and many times when we are reading, or when a preacher or teacher is speaking, it is as if the words burn within us and are being directed to us personally. They fit our circumstances so much it is just as if they were spoken out loud in our spirit, and the Holy Spirit bears witness the Lord is speaking to us through that person.

**God sometimes communicates his direction as a desire.** The Holy Spirit puts those desires in our heart. "Delight yourself also in the Lord, and He shall give you the desires of your heart. Commit your way to the Lord, trust also in Him, and He shall bring it to pass."[125]

**Sometimes we have a desire, an impression or an inclination** to do something that we had not previously thought to do. You will know which way to go whenever you turn to the right hand or whenever you turn to the left. Your ears shall hear a word behind you, saying, "This is the way, walk in it."[126]

As we read and study God's Word, it is stored in our sub-conscience. In a time of crisis, the Holy Spirit will bring back to remembrance a verse of Scripture we did not even know we knew, one that we certainly did not remember, but it will be just the right advice. "These things I have spoken to you while being present with you. But the Helper, the Holy Spirit, whom the Father will send in My name, He will teach you all things, and bring to your remembrance all things that I said to you."[127]

The Bible promises the Holy Spirit will help us when we don't know what or how to pray and make intercession for us to be able to face our crisis. "Likewise the Spirit also helps our infirmities: for we know not what we should pray for as we ought: but the Spirit itself makes intercession for us with groanings which cannot be uttered. And he that searches the heart makes intercession for the saints according to the will of God."[128]

**God speaks to us through our thoughts.** When we are thinking about a problem, there are times when a thought comes into our minds that did not originate with us. We must ask ourselves, "Where did that thought originate?" Thoughts that come into our minds that are in agreement with the Word of God are God speaking to us in our thoughts. Until we know the Word of God, we will have a difficult time knowing if what we hear is the voice of God, the devil, or our own thoughts, because the devil also puts thoughts in our minds. The devil's thoughts will not line up with the Word of God. They will appeal to our flesh.

Here is a good yardstick to test if you are hearing from God: If you are walking in the Spirit (being obedient to God), usually the first thought you have is from God and your second thought is from the devil. If you are walking in the flesh (not being obedient to God), the first thought is usually from the devil and your second thought is from God.

Example 1: The Holy Spirit might tell you to give $500.00 to someone in need, and the devil will immediately tell you that you can't afford to do so.

Example 2: The devil might tell you to retaliate when you suffer a wrong, but the Holy Spirit will remind you that you are to do good and pray for those who mistreat you.

**God speaks to us through the prompting of the Holy Spirit.** The Helper, who is the Holy Spirit, will bring to our remembrance all things Jesus has spoken to us through His Word. He guides Christians in numerous ways by convicting them of sins, revealing God's truths, teaching God's ways, and reinforcing Christ's words. The Spirit helps Christians testify to the truth of Christ when they are witnessing to unbelievers by giving them God's words to speak. He also reveals the Father's thoughts and helps believers know how to pray. All of this takes place in our hearts and in our minds.

**God speaks to us so clearly sometimes we almost think it is audible.** In the Bible, 1 Samuel chapter three, the story is recorded about Eli and Samuel. The LORD called Samuel: and he answered, "Here am I." Samuel thought three times it was Eli calling him, but Eli said it was not him, but the Lord. Then there is the story of Elijah in the book of 1 Kings. He was discouraged, and he looked for God's voice in the wind, but God was not in the wind. He looked for God in the earthquake, but God was not in the earthquake. Then there was a fire, but God was not in the fire. Last came a gentle wind blowing, and through that gentle breeze came God's still soft voice.

**Many times God speaks to us in the stillness.** Psalms 46:10 says "Be still, and know that I am God." Turn off all the noises and listen. Many times we have so much noise going on around us we can't think. Certainly we can not hear God's voice amid the clamor.

**God speaks through other Believers.** God uses His people to give us His message. "Now then, we are ambassadors for Christ; it is as though God were pleading through us: we implore you on Christ's behalf, be reconciled to God."[129]

**God uses others to give us counsel.** "Where there is no counsel, the people fall; but in the multitude of counselors there is safety."[130]

Many people only take their problems to other people to solve instead of taking them to God, and this can cause them problems. We should take our problems to God first and ask for wisdom. We need to remember God loves us more than any human we know. Sometimes the worst counsel is from the ones we love the most. We always must weigh counsel from others to see if the counsel lines up with how we believe God is directing us.

**God speaks to His people through circumstances.** Repeatedly, in the Old Testament God spoke to His people through circumstances. We know when we are praying for God to move, if a door of opportunity opens we must go through at once. If it closes we know this is a door He doesn't want us to walk through at this time, for reasons we may or may not understand. In these circumstances, we must believe our Father knows best.

**God assures us by the peace we feel.** When we pray and make our petitions known, His peace descends upon us. We know He has heard and is saying everything will be alright.

Philippians 4:6-7 tells us "Be anxious for nothing, but in everything by prayer and supplication, with thanksgiving, let your requests be made known unto God; and the peace of God, which passes all understanding, shall keep your hearts and minds through Christ Jesus."

When we pray, the peace of God will invade our being and we will be anxious for nothing.

We need to remember that there is not a formula for how God will speak, but there are guidelines to give us direction and guidance. After we pray, four things must be in alignment for us to know we are hearing from God:

- **What we hear will be in agreement with the Word of God.**

- **The circumstances will line up with His direction.**

- **You will be prompted by the Holy Spirit in your mind the right decision to make.**

- **You will have the peace of God in your heart after you make your decision.**

It is interesting to listen to other people's testimonies of how God spoke to them in a certain circumstance. We can all benefit from the rich experience and wisdom of other believers. God's voice is unique for every one; this is why testimonies are so powerful. They help increase our faith. Just remember, God probably will not speak to you the same way He did to someone else!

As we read the following scriptures, listen to how many times God speaks through His word. We are commanded to listen, and look also at the many benefits we receive when we listen and obey God's voice.

Exodus 15:25 "There He made a statute and an ordinance for them, and there He tested them, and said, 'If you diligently heed the voice of the LORD your God and do what is right in His sight, give ear to His commandments and keep all His statutes, I will put none of the diseases on you which I have brought on the Egyptians. I am the LORD who heals you.'"

Psalms 78:1 "Give ear, O my people, to my law; Incline your ears to the words of my mouth."

Proverbs 2:1-12 "My son, if you receive my words, And treasure my commands within you, so that you incline your ear to wisdom, And apply your heart to understanding; Yes, if you cry out for discernment, And lift up your voice for understanding, If you seek her as silver, And search for her as for hidden treasures; Then you will understand the fear of the LORD, And find the knowledge of God. For the LORD gives wisdom; From His mouth come knowledge and understanding; He stores up sound wisdom for the upright; He is a shield to those who walk uprightly; He guards the paths of justice, and preserves the way of His saints. Then you will understand righteousness and justice, Equity and every good path. When wisdom enters your heart, and knowledge is pleasant to your soul, Discretion will preserve you; Understanding will keep you, to deliver you from the way of evil, from the man who speaks perverse things."

Proverbs 5:1 "My son, pay attention to my wisdom; Lend your ear to my understanding."

Matthew 13:9,13-17 "Who hath ears to hear, let him hear . . . Therefore I speak to them in parables, because seeing they do not see, and hearing they do not hear, nor do they understand. And in them the prophecy of Isaiah is fulfilled, which says: 'Hearing you will hear and shall not understand, and seeing you will see and not perceive; For the hearts of this people have grown dull. Their ears are hard of hearing, and their eyes they have closed, lest they should see with their eyes and hear with their ears, lest they should understand with their hearts and turn, So that I should heal them.' But blessed are your eyes for they see, and your ears for they hear; for assuredly, I say to you that many prophets and righteous men desired to see what you see, and did not see it, and to hear what you hear, and did not hear it."

Matthew 13:18-23 "Therefore hear the parable of the sower: When anyone hears the word of the kingdom, and does not understand it, then the wicked one comes and snatches away what was sown in his heart. This is he who received seed by the wayside. But he who received the seed on stony places, this is he who hears the word and immediately receives it with joy; yet he has no root in himself, but endures only for a while. For when tribulation or persecution arises because of the word, immediately he stumbles. Now he who received seed among the thorns is he, who hears the word, and the cares of this world and the deceitfulness of riches choke the word, and he becomes unfruitful. But he who received seed on the good ground is he who hears the word and understands it, who indeed bears fruit and produces: some a hundredfold, some sixty, some thirty."

Revelation 2:7 "He who has an ear, let him hear what the Spirit says to the churches. To him who overcomes I will give to eat from the tree of life, which is in the midst of the Paradise of God."'

Verse 11 "He that hath an ear let him hear what the Spirit says unto the churches. He that overcomes shall not be hurt of the second death."

Verse 17 "He that hath an ear let him hear what the Spirit says unto the churches. To him that overcomes will I give to eat of the hidden manna, and will give him a white stone, and in the stone a new name written, which no man knows except he that receives it."

Verse 26 "And he that overcomes, and keeps my works unto the end, to him will I give power over the nations—'He shall rule them with a rod of iron; as the vessels of a potter shall they be broken to shivers'—even as I received of my Father. And I will give him the morning star. He that hath an ear let him hear what the Spirit says unto the churches."

## The differences between Satan's voice and God's voice:

| | |
|---|---|
| Satan lies. | God cannot lie. |
| Satan offers shortcuts. | God offers the narrow way. |
| Satan justifies sin. | God calls for repentance. |
| Satan divides. | God unites. |
| Satan fosters pride. | God brings humility. |
| Satan excuses the means to an end. | God requires integrity. |
| Satan tries to make you hurry. | God says, "Wait." |

## What things keep people from hearing God's voice?

- **Satan lies, telling people God doesn't speak to them.**
- **They do not know God.**
- **Only born again people hear from God.**
- **Unbelief: they are not trained to know they hear from God.**
- **Poor Self Esteem: they don't believe they are good enough.**
- **Doubt and unbelief that God will speak to them.**
- **Guilt because they know they have rebelled and refused to obey what God has told them.**
- **A rebellious spirit: they turn deaf ears to what He is saying.**

- **God directed anger: they are mad with God for something that has happened to them so they are resisting, stifling, or grieving the Holy Spirit.**

- **Harboring sin: holding on to a sin that God's word tells them to give up.**

- **Busy-ness: not providing an atmosphere in which they could hear Him speak, if He should.**

- **They reject the person through whom God speaks.**

## How to hear from God:

- **Make sure you have repented of your sins, confessed with your mouth, and believed in your heart that Jesus Christ died to set you free from your sins, and have asked Him to be the Lord of your life.**

- **Believe God speaks to you because the Bible says he does.**

- **Always obey what the Bible tells you to do.**

- **Always obey when a preacher or teacher gives you God's Word, not because of the preacher's word, but because God's Word says for you to obey.**

- **Do not resist, stifle, or grieve the Holy Spirit.**

- **Ask God to show you any sin He wants you to give up that you have not been willing to give up.**

- **Turn off the radio, the TV, the telephone, and anything else which distracts you.**

- **Ask God to speak to you.**

- **Believe you hear from God and you will hear from God!**

What a blessed assurance we experience when we know we hear from God. When we learn to recognize His voice, do what He says, and enjoy fellowship with Him, it brings us joy unspeakable.

# Chapter 17

## HOW CAN A PERSON KNOW GOD'S WILL?

All of us want to know God's will for our lives, but how many of us want to do God's will? How many of us know what His will for our lives is? I personally have not heard many sermons preached on knowing God's will. I must admit to you, until I began studying to know God's will, I confused the will of God with God's guidance. I would seek God's will, when what I needed to do was seek God's guidance. So what's the difference?

### What is God's will and how can we know it?

"For where there is a testament (will), there must also of necessity be the death of the testator. For a testament (will) is in force after men are dead, since it has no power at all while the testator lives."[131]

When a man or woman dies, they leave their heirs their last will and testament, or their last wishes. After Jesus Christ died, we received His "last will and testament." The New Testament is filled with God's will for our lives. His commandments found within the New Testament are His will for us to follow if we want to enter into the Kingdom of Heaven, become sons of God, and joint heirs with Jesus Christ. Therefore, we must look to the Bible to find God's will for our lives.

"For I know the thoughts that I think toward you, says the LORD, thoughts of peace and not of evil, to give you a hope and a future."[132] God has a plan for our lives and if we will obey and trust Him, He will bring it to pass.

**John 6:38-40** "I have come down from heaven, not to do My own will, but the will of Him who sent Me. This is the will of the Father who sent Me, that of all He has given Me I should lose nothing, but should raise it up at the last day. And this is the will of Him who sent Me that everyone who sees the Son and believes in Him may have everlasting life; and I will raise him up at the last day." It is God's will that everyone who believes in the Son will have everlasting life, and be raised up on the last day.

**Galatians 1:4** "Jesus gave Himself for our sins that He might deliver us from this present evil age, according to the will of our God and Father, to whom be glory forever and ever. Amen." It is God's will to deliver us from this present evil age.

**Ephesians 1:**3-6 "Blessed be the God and Father of our Lord Jesus Christ, who has blessed us with every spiritual blessing in the heavenly places in Christ, just as He chose us in Him before the foundation of the world, that we should be holy and without blame before Him in love, having predestined us to adoption as sons by Jesus Christ to Himself, according to the good pleasure of His will, to the praise of the glory of His grace, by which He made us accepted in the Beloved." It is God's will to adopt us as sons by Jesus Christ and bless us with every spiritual blessing that we would be holy and without blame before Him in love.

**Romans 12:2** "Do not be conformed to this world, but be transformed by the renewing of your mind, that you may prove what is that good and acceptable and perfect will of God." It is God's will that we be transformed by the renewing of our minds. Then we will know His will.

We have talked about the triune being of man. The natural man is made up of his mind, his emotions, and his will. In this scripture we are told to be transformed by the renewing of our minds. After we have been born again, it is imperative that we have our thinking changed; if we don't change our thinking we will continue to act just like we did before we were born again. As we begin to study the Word of God, we find that it is 180 degrees different than our ways. God says, "My ways are not your ways." God seldom does things the way we think He should.

Our emotions dictate our moods, whether we are happy or sad. They dictate when our feelings are hurt; they dictate how we feel about ourselves. We feel we have no control over them, dismissing them by saying, "God just made me this way." We have seen when people live in the flesh; sometimes their emotions rule them all their lives with jealousy, envy, and bitterness. The older they get the worse their dispositions seem to become. Our new creature is not to live out of our emotions, but out of our will. We have previously said, "When a person becomes born again, big "I" must be dethroned." Our will must be replaced by God's will. It has been said, "Pure religion resides in the will alone," meaning the will is the governing power of our actions. If the will is set right, our actions must come into harmony with our will. By this it does not mean the wish of the man, or even his purpose, but the deliberate choice of the will. The will of man is the deciding power, the king, to which all that is in the man must yield obedience. We sometimes feel our emotions are the governing power, but we all realize as a matter of practical experience that there is something within us, behind our emotions and wishes, an independent self that decides everything and controls our minds, our thoughts and actions.

Our emotions belong to us, and are suffered and enjoyed by us, but they are not who we are; and if God is to take possession of us, it must be into this central will or personality that He enters. If then, He is reigning there by the power of His Spirit, all the rest of our nature must come under His sway; and as the will is, so is the man.

**1 Thessalonians 5:16** Rejoice always, pray without ceasing, in everything give thanks; for this is the will of God in Christ Jesus for you.

This is one of the scriptures by which I have patterned my life. I believe whatever happens is the will of God for my life, and I can thank Him in the midst of my trial. I do not become alarmed when things don't go as I planned. If my schedule or my life has to be adjusted, it is because He has a better plan. He promises and I believe that all things work together for my good because I have been called according to God's purposes. Many times I do not understand, but afterwards I can see God's hand in the circumstances. This has worked for me for over fifty years.

**We have been taught that man has a free will. This means he is free to choose his actions.**

**Deuteronomy 5:29** Oh that they had such a heart in them that they would fear Me and always keep all My commandments that it might be well with them and with their children forever!

We see from this verse we have a free will, or a choice. God is saying that we can have such a heart in ourselves if we want one. He wants us to keep His commandments so that it would be well for us and our children forever. In Deuteronomy 30:19 God says we can either choose life or death. If I have a choice, I will choose life!

**Isaiah 1:18-20** "'Come now, and let us reason together,' says the LORD, 'Though your sins are like scarlet, they shall be as white as snow; though they are red like crimson, they shall be as wool. If you are willing and obedient you shall eat the good of the land; But if you refuse and rebel, you shall be devoured by the sword,' for the mouth of the LORD has spoken." God is saying "if" you are obedient. This again, implies we have a choice or will in the matter.

## How important is it to do His will?

**Matthew 7:21-27** "Not everyone who says to Me, 'Lord, Lord,' shall enter the kingdom of heaven, but he who does the will of My Father in heaven. Many will say to Me in that day, 'Lord, Lord, have we not prophesied in Your name, cast out demons in Your name, and done many wonders in Your name?' And then I will declare to them, 'I never knew you; depart from Me, you who practice lawlessness!' Therefore whoever hears these sayings of Mine, and does them, I will liken him to a wise man who built his house on the rock: and the rain descended, the floods came, and the winds blew and beat on that house; and it did not fall, for it was founded on the rock. But everyone who hears these sayings of Mine, and does not do them, will be like a foolish man who built his house on the sand: and the rain descended, the floods came, and the winds blew and beat on that house; and it fell. And great was its fall."

**Matthew 12:50 & Mark 3:35** "For whoever does the will of My Father in heaven is My brother and sister and mother."

## Jesus did the will of the Father and we are to do the same.

**Philippians 2:5** "Let this mind be in you which was also in Christ Jesus, 6who, being in the form of God, did not consider it robbery to be equal with God."

**Mark 14:36 & Luke 22:42** "Take this cup away from Me; nevertheless, not what I will, but what You will."

**Luke 11:2 & Matthew 6:9** "So He said to them, 'When you pray, say: Our Father in heaven, Hallowed be Your name. Your kingdom come. Your will be done on earth as it is in heaven.'"

**John 4:34** "Jesus said to them, 'My food is to do the will of Him who sent Me, and to finish His work.'"

**John 5:30** "I can of Myself do nothing. As I hear, I judge; and My judgment is righteous, because I do not seek My own will but the will of the Father who sent Me."

From the above Scriptures, we can see it is vitally important to do the will of God. We have a choice: we can determine to set our wills according to the Word of God or determine we will do what pleases us.

## So what is the practical application of doing God's will?

Since man's will is really the man's self, what his will decides, he does. Your part then is simply to put your will in accordance with the Word of God, which is God's will. You get on God's side, making up your mind that you will believe what His word says because He says it, and you will not pay any regard to the feelings that make it seem so unreal. God will not fail to respond, sooner or later, with His revelation to such a faith.

**1 Corinthians 7:37** "Nevertheless he who stands steadfast in his heart, having no necessity, but has power over his own will, and has so determined in his heart does well."

**John 7:17** "Jesus answered them and said, 'My doctrine is not Mine, but His who sent Me. If anyone wills to do His will, he shall know concerning the doctrine, whether it is from God or whether I speak on My own authority.'"

**Philippians 2:13** "It is God who works in you both to will and to do for His good pleasure." When we determine to obey Him, he helps us do His will and uses us for His good pleasure."

**Ephesians 4:22-24** "You put off, concerning your former conduct, the old man which grows corrupt according to the deceitful lusts, and be renewed in the spirit of your mind, and you put on the new man which was created according to God, in true righteousness and holiness."

**Philippians 2:5-8** "Let this mind be in you which was also in Christ Jesus, who, being in the form of God, did not consider it robbery to be equal with God, but made Himself of no reputation, taking the form of a bondservant, and coming in the likeness of men. And being found in appearance as a man, He humbled Himself and became obedient to the point of death, even the death of the cross."

**2 Corinthians 8:10-12** "It is to your advantage not only to be doing what you began and were desiring to do a year ago, but now you also must complete the doing of it; that as there was a readiness to desire it, so there also may be a completion out of what you have. If there is first a willing mind, it is accepted according to what one has, and not according to what he does not have."

As an example, when we first hear we are supposed to forgive, our emotions balk at forgiving those who have hurt us or done so much harm. We must choose, or set our will, to forgive and believe that God will do what he says. The Bible says, "If we confess our sins He is faithful and just to forgive us and to cleanse us from all sins."[133] Un-forgiveness is a sin. As we set our will to forgive, the Holy Spirit who lives inside us does the work that we cannot do without His help, and in a few days you will find yourself triumphant, with every emotion and every thought brought into captivity to the power of the Spirit of God, who has taken possession of your will that was put into His hands.

The secret of doing God's will lies here: our will which determines our actions, has been under the control of sin and self. We have said and done things we regret, which seemingly we had no control over. Now God calls upon us to yield our wills unto Him, that He may take control of them, and may work in us to will and to do of His good pleasure. If we will obey this call, and present ourselves to Him as a living sacrifice, He will take possession of our surrendered wills and begin at once to work in us that which is well pleasing in His sight, through Jesus Christ, giving us the mind that was in Christ and transforming us into His image.

As a much younger Christian, I had a besetting sin, which in my emotions made me feel good, but in my will I hated. I did not realize I had control over my emotions. I found myself unable to conquer the feelings and struggled with my emotions, which I thought should first be changed. But I learned this secret concerning my will and going to God I said, "Lord you see that with my emotions, I love this sin, but in my

157

real central self, I hate it. Until now my emotions have had the mastery; but now I put my will into your hands, and give it up to your working. I will never again consent, in my will, to yield to this sin. Take possession of my will, and work in me to will and to do of your good pleasure. Immediately I began to find deliverance. The Lord took possession of my will as I surrendered to Him and began to work by His power, so that His will in the matter gained the mastery over my emotions. I found myself delivered, not by the power of an outward commandment, but by the inward power of the Spirit of God working in me that which was well pleasing in His sight.

Because of certain events, another day I found myself harboring a terrible emotion of hatred. I had never experienced such a horrible, vile thing. I willed myself to walk in the spirit, but this was beyond my ability to control. Without God's help I knew I was going to allow this emotion to rule me. At a prayer meeting I asked the ladies to pray asking God to remove this hatred from me because I knew I couldn't handle it on my own. If I had allowed this emotion (which rose up to dominate my life) to overtake me and had rebelled against doing God's will of being forgiving and loving, I would have been in utter despair. But I had learned this secret of the will, and knowing that, at the bottom, I really chose the will of God, I knew the emotion had to line up with the Word of God. In the face of all my rebelling feelings, I submitted my will to God's. The result was that in an incredibly short space of time, every thought was brought into captivity, and I began to find the hatred gone. The hatred which I surrendered was replaced with love and compassion for the person. I was able to rejoice in being able to do the will of God. What a victory!

Let's look at how to apply this principle to our lives. Put aside your emotions. Don't let your emotions rule what you do, they are only the servants; and regard simply your will, which is the real "king" in your being. Does your will choose to obey; does your will choose to decide to believe? If this is the case then you are in the Lord's hands. As we will to do His will, God works in us both to will and work things for His good pleasure, and we find ourselves doing the will of God that our emotions said we could never do.

We have looked at God's will. Now let's take a look at seeking guidance to do his will in our decision-making. We must establish the fact that God will give us guidance, and we must believe He does. Let us look to God's Word to establish this fact.

**John 10:3-4** "To him the doorkeeper opens, and the sheep hear his voice; and he calls his own sheep by name and leads them out. And when he brings out his own sheep, he goes before them; and the sheep follow him, for they know his voice."

**John 14:26** "But the Helper, the Holy Spirit, whom the Father will send in My name, He will teach you all things, and bring to your remembrance all things that I said to you."

**James 1:5** "If any of you lacks wisdom, let him ask of God, who gives to all liberally and without reproach, and it will be given to him."

With such declarations as these and many more, we must believe that Divine guidance is promised to us. Our faith must therefore confidently look for and expect His guidance. This is essential for in James 1:6-8 we read "Let him ask in faith, with no doubting, for he who doubts is like a wave of the sea driven and tossed by the wind. Let not that man suppose that he will receive anything from the Lord; he is a double-minded man, unstable in all his ways.

So let's settle this point: divine guidance has been promised. If you seek it, you are sure to receive it. This is a good place to begin willing yourself to believe. Say to yourself, "I choose to believe! I choose to believe!" We have just studied that it is God who works in us to will and do of His good pleasure.

There are four ways in which God reveals His guidance to us:

- **Through the Scripture**
- **Through providential circumstances**
- **Through convictions of our own higher judgment (which is the Holy Spirit in us)**
- **Through the inward peace we feel when the decision is made**

Someone has said all of these must be in complete harmony and then you will know it is the will of God for you in your circumstance.

If you are in doubt about your situation, you must first of all consult the Bible and see whether there is any law there to direct you. Until you have found and obeyed God's will as it is there revealed, you must not ask nor expect a separate, direct, personal revelation. If God has already given us explicit directions about something in His Word, He will not of course make a special revelation to us about that thing. If you do not find any principles that will settle your point, or difficulty, then you must consider another way mentioned. We have to be very careful about making our decisions based on the circumstances and our own understanding. Circumstances can cloud our thinking. Family and friends, who may not be walking in the Spirit, can influence our own human, unenlightened understanding. Never take any guidance from anyone unless it is in your heart to do what they say. Pastor Peter Lord said, "If you are not born again, the first thoughts you have about a situation are from the devil and your second thoughts are from God. If you are born again, the first thoughts you have are from God and the second thoughts are from the devil." If any of these tests fail, it is not safe to proceed. Please do not get involved in anything in which you do not have evidence that God is in. If you feel God wants you to do something say, "Lord, how do I know that You are present?" Some people pray for open or closed doors, which I have used on many occasions. When God opens the way or closes the door say, "Thank you, Lord, for showing me the way."

Doors are closed by: Circumstances, other people, Satan, and God. In Matthew we have already seen that Jesus is the doorkeeper, and in Revelations He opens the doors that no man can shut. So Jesus is the guardian of doors. Sometimes the door closes, and you can not do what you had planned on doing.

### So why does God allow closed doors in our lives?

**To protect us from making a mistake or a wrong decision**

**To redirect us for a greater opportunity, service, fruitfulness, satisfaction, or glory**

**To test our faith as it teaches us to trust Him**

**To build perseverance in our lives**

**To better equip us**

**The time is not right**

**Maybe because of disobedience or sins of the past**

**It could be you rebelled against God and you closed the door yourself by:**

- **Taking matters into your own hands**

- **Harboring anger, bitterness, or resentment**

- **Blaming others instead of taking personal responsibility**

- **Being cold toward God**

God is never late . . . but He doesn't always come on our time. He has His reasons. He is doing something in us while we wait.

In Psalms 37:4-5 we read, "Delight yourself also in the LORD, and He shall give you the desires of your heart. Commit your way to the LORD, trust also in Him, and He shall bring it to pass."

Philippians 2:13 "It is God who works in you both to will and to do for His good pleasure.

This means that He will take possession of our will and work in such a way that His suggestions will come to us, not so much commands from the outside, as desires springing up within. Take all your present perplexities, then, to the Lord. Tell Him you only want to know and obey His voice, and ask Him to make it plain to you. Promise Him that you will obey whatever it may be. Believe implicitly that He is guiding you, according to His word. In all doubtful things, wait for clear light. Look and listen for His voice continually; and the moment you are sure, then, but not until then, yield and obey immediately. Trust Him to make you forget the impression if it is not His will. If it continues and is in harmony with all His other guidance, do not be afraid to obey.

Above all else, trust Him. Nowhere is faith more needed than here. He has promised to guide. You have asked Him to do it. Now you must believe that He does, and take what comes as being His guidance. God cannot guide those souls who do not trust Him enough to believe He is guiding them. He never asks us to do anything that ultimately is not for our good, and His guidance will give us joy unspeakable!

# Chapter 18

## WHAT IS BETTY'S TESTIMONY?

W hen I first began to hear people's testimonies back in the sixties, I was awed! I said, "Lord I almost wish I had gone through some of the awful things I hear about because these people seem to love you more than me." He said, "You should love me more because you didn't have to go through them!" I could tell you many things which have happened to me that God brought me through, but more importantly I want to tell you what He taught me.

I accepted Him as my Savior when I was nine years old, and He guarded and protected me during my youth until I was married at the age of twenty. Proverbs 1:8-9 says: "My son, hear the instruction of your father, And do not forsake the law of your mother; for they will be a graceful ornament on your head, and chains about your neck." My parents' instructions kept me from going the way of the world. This taught me why it is so important for us to teach our children obedience, so that it will be easier for them to learn obedience to God. He is a God who guards and protects us. **That was the God of my yesterdays.**

I could tell you God allowed me to marry the man of my dreams, my prince charming; and how I later found out that marriage is not a fairy tale. Instead, I will tell you that our God will teach us how to live with and love our mates if we ask Him. He is a God that teaches us how to love. **That was the God of my yesterdays.**

I could tell you of washing my clothes one Saturday back in 1955 and hanging them out to dry. They weren't dry at nightfall, so I left them out. Someone stole them that night. We had few clothes, no money, and no insurance. I prayed, without much faith, but really hoping that we would get our clothes back. There were thousands of people in Savannah in 1955; what happened the following week was unbelievable. I left my office to go to the bank to make a deposit. I was returning to the office on the elevator when I saw a woman wearing my clothes, standing next to me. Not knowing what to do, I got off at my stop which was on the third floor. My co-workers suggested I try to find where she went. I went to the fourth and final floor occupied by a real estate office. The clerk told me she had paid her rent so I was able to get her name and address. I told my husband the details of who she was and where she lived. The police went to her home and within an hour all my clothes had been returned. And I thought "Wasn't that luck! What a coincidence!" I was so unaware of how God works—I wasn't even aware that He had answered my prayer! **That was the God of my yesterdays.**

I could tell you of finding myself as a new bride dealing with a lot of insecurities, jealousy, envy, hurt feelings, feeling as if I were being overworked, underpaid and acting like a selfish spoiled brat, but I'm not going to tell you about that. I am going to tell you that God loved me so much He helped me deal with all of my problems when I took them to Him. Our God delivers us from all our besetting sins! I began to see that God hears us when we pray. Praise God! We serve a God who answers prayers. **That was the God of my yesterdays.**

I could tell you of being a young adult and letting every excuse keep me from attending Sunday school and church. Instead, I am going to tell you that my husband and I were facing an insurmountable problem, and we needed a miracle. Even when God had been so wonderful to answer all the prayers about which I have told you, I didn't recognize Him. I thought it was luck or a coincidence! I told my husband, "I have heard that if you pray believing, God will answer your prayer." I told God that if He would answer my prayer, I would get back in church where I belonged. Within two weeks God had answered my prayer, and this time I knew it was a miracle! I have missed few Sundays since 1958! I then knew that we have a God that answers prayers, and I knew that what I thought was luck or coincidence was God working miracles in my life! We serve a miracle working God!! **That was the God of my yesterdays.**

I could tell you the ordeal of my beautiful six year old daughter suddenly losing her eyesight, my husband's subsequent salvation, and my daughter's eyesight being miraculous restored. Instead, I want you to know we serve a miracle working God who gives peace and great comfort in the time of need. **That was the God of my yesterdays.**

I could tell you of having to deal with the rebellion of that same daughter when she was fifteen years old. Instead, I will tell you that God taught me that we have authority over Satan. We can rebuke him and he has to flee! We serve a God who gives us the tools we need to win every spiritual battle! **That was the God of my yesterdays.**

I could tell you of operating a business with my husband and the difficulties and hardships we faced. Instead, I will tell you that our miraculous God met our every need even when I thought it was impossible. Not only that, once when the storms of life were all around me, I experienced calm I had never had before. I knew the application was spiritual, and I looked it up in the Bible. It is Psalms 107:25-31. "For He commands and raises the stormy wind, which lifts up the waves of the sea. They mount up to the heavens, they go down again to the depths; their soul melts because of trouble. They reel to and fro, and stagger like a drunken man, and are at their wit's end. Then they cry out to the Lord in their trouble, and He brings them out of their distresses. He calms the storm, so that its waves are still. Then they are glad because they are quiet; So He guides them to their desired haven. Oh, that men would give thanks to the Lord for His goodness, and for His wonderful works to the children of men!" Instead, I want to tell you our God gives peace in the midst of the storm and He does bring us to our desired haven. What a mighty God we serve!! Oh that men would give thanks to the Lord for His goodness and for His wonderful works to the children of men! **That was the God of my yesterdays.**

I wish I had time to tell you of selling our business, paying off all we owed, taking a second mortgage from the buyer, which would have given us a healthy income for the next fifteen years, and in six months having the buyer go bankrupt with us having no recourse. I could tell you of trying to live on only my husband's social security with a car payment of $429.00 every month, and having nothing to depend on except God. It is absolutely amazing what God did to provide. Instead, I will tell you this, "If that is what I had to go through to learn that we have a God on whom we can depend in a crisis and that with His help we don't have to worry, praise Him for His goodness and His wonderful works to the children of men!" **That was the God of my yesterdays.**

Some of you have lost your loved ones and husbands, and some of you still have that to face. When I lost my mother in 1965, I had never lost anyone dear to me. Before her death, I thought I would not be able to face the future without Mom and Dad. Yet when she died, God spoke to me as I viewed her in her casket, "That's not your Mother—to be absent from the body is to be present with the Lord. Your mother's body is here, but her spirit is with Me! You were a good daughter to her so you have nothing to cry about but your own selfishness, but it is o.k. to cry because you will miss her." I was overjoyed that God would speak such comforting words to me at the worst time of my life. It took all my fears away! How awesome is that!

We have all heard that God gives us peace that passes all understanding and I had experienced peace, but I had never experienced peace that I couldn't understand until I lost my beloved husband of almost fifty-five years. A peace, calmness, and a lack of fear came over me that passed all my understanding. We serve a God who can give joy and peace as we walk through the valley of the shadow of death and we need fear no evil. What a great and mighty God we serve!! Oh, that men would praise Him for His goodness and His wonderful works to the children of men! **That was the God of my yesterdays.**

In the past three years, I have found myself questioning my life and my decisions, and today I am finding out things I never even knew about myself. I want you to know that God is still answering my prayers today. He still speaks to me in my mind, He speaks to me today through His servants, he speaks to me today through His Word, and He speaks to me today through circumstances and the peace that only He can give. Today I am one of the most blessed people you will ever meet. His mercies are new every morning, and He wants to fellowship with us. He has proved Himself worthy of my praise, my adoration, my love, my loyalty, and my commitment. Oh, that men would praise Him for His goodness and His wonderful works to the children of men! **This is my God of today!**

We live in very uncertain times. If we aren't careful, we will allow the news media, or people, to put fear in our hearts concerning the future of our country and even the world system as we know it. Praise be to God that He is all knowing, all powerful and a very present help in the time of trouble. If we are His children, we can call on Him today, right now, whether we are rich or poor, sick or in health, and He will hear us. Do you belong to Him? Do you know Him as the God of yesterday? Do you know Him as the God of today? If not, He longs for you to know him today. **This is my God of Today!**

Hopefully, my thoughts of how God was there for me yesterday through answered prayers and miracles will help you to see the character of our loving God. He helps us fight our battles and sets us free from doubt, fear and worry. He is an ever present help in the time of trouble and knowing how He is able to give us joy and peace in the midst of every crisis will stir up memories of how great God has been for you in your yesterdays. Knowing how much He loves us today, I pray we will all feel like David when he faced Goliath. David was so sure that God had been with him in his yesterdays that he had no doubt God would be with him in his present when he faced the giant Goliath! We know God is faithful and no respecter of persons. What He has done for others, He will do for us!

More importantly, if you are not a Christian, you are missing out on a wonderful life! Tell the heavenly Father that you are a sinner and that you have really made a mess of your life trying to do things your way. Invite God to come into your life and take over. Oh, the peace and contentment you will feel! **This is the God of our tomorrows!**

It is my prayer that we can all say with assurance, "I don't know what my tomorrows hold—but I know who holds my tomorrows." I am now—and I will be alright!

**This is my God of yesterdays, today, tomorrow and forever! Amen!**

# FOR ME

On that wooden cross, the blessed
Savior died.
Pouring out His life's blood
For sinners, He was crucified.

Sinners who are black with sin,
Beautiful outside, yet so ugly within.
I was one of those for whom the
Savior died.
I was one for whom He was crucified.

In one of those intimate moments
Alone with Him,
He spoke to me, the real me, the
One within.
"I died so that you might live."

Oh, what a sobering thought!
It was through His blood, that I was bought!
Then He so gently said to me:

"Now you too must die,
not on a cruel cross—but daily to self,
so that you may be a reflection of me
and my love to a world that's lost."

Written by Betty W. O'Berry 11/21/89

# Endnotes

1. Psalms 14:1
2. Romans 1:20
3. Hebrews 11:6
4. Civilization Past & Present, Vol. I Page 31, Wallbank & Raylor
5. James 4:12
6. Genesis 1:1
7. Job 19:25
8. Deuteronomy 18:11-12
9. Genesis 2:7
10. Ezekiel 37:9
11. 1 Samuel 10:10
12. Matthew 3:13, Mark 1:9, Luke 3:21
13. Luke 4:14
14. Acts 2:16-18
15. Romans 8:9
16. Ephesians 5:18
17. Galatians 5:22
18. 1 Corinthians 12, 13, & 14
19. Deuteronomy 18:11-12
20. Hosea 4:4
21. Colossians 1:16
22. James 4:17
23. 1 John 3:4
24. Exodus 20
25. Mathew 22:36-40
26. Romans 14:23
27. 1 John 5:17
28. Romans 1:28-32
29. Galatians 5:19
30. Genesis 2:16-17
31. Genesis 3:16
32. Romans 6:16
33. John 8:44
34. Matthew 4:1-3
35. Romans 5: 12 & 18
36. Romans 3:10 &23
37. Ezekiel 18:4
38. Isaiah 59:2
39. James 2:26
40. Matthew 12:34
41. Proverbs 4:23
42. Jeremiah 1:5
43. John 3:6
44. Psalms 8:4-8
45. Genesis 1:26-28
46. Genesis 2:7
47. Genesis 2:16-17
48. Romans 5:12
49. Romans 6:16
50. John 8:44
51. John 3:6
52. Romans 8:8
53. 1 Corinthians 15:44
54. Romans 8:6-7
55. 1 Corinthians 2:14
56. Ephesians 4:22
57. Proverbs 22:15
58. James 1:5
59. Galatians 5:19
60. John 17:17
61. John 8:32
62. Romans 10:14-17
63. Romans 1:16-17

64. John 5:24
65. Matthew 18:3
66. Romans 3:23-25
67. Hebrews 9:22
68. Isaiah 64:6
69. Romans 7:24
70. John 3:3-21
71. John 6:40
72. John 3:16
73. John 11:25-26
74. John 1:12-13
75. Romans 10:13
76. Hebrews 11:6
77. 2 Corinthians 5:17 & 21
78. Ephesians 2:1-3
79. Ephesians 4:22
80. Acts 2:37-39
81. Acts 3:19
82. Mark 16:16
83. Romans 6:3-14
84. Romans 10:9-10
85. Ephesians 2:4-10
86. 2 Corinthians 5:7
87. 2 Corinthians 5:17-21
88. Romans 8:14-15
89. Hebrews 2:14-15
90. Ephesians 4:22-24
91. Ephesians 1:3-6
92. 1 Corinthians 1:7-8
93. Isaiah 40:31
94. Hebrews 9:12-14
95. Romans 12:2
96. 1 Corinthians 2:14
97. John 4:24
98. 1 Corinthians 12:3

99. James 3:9-11
100. Galatians 5:22-23
101. Matthew 6:14
102. Matthew 6:8
103. 1 Thessalonians 5:16
104. 1 John 4:7-8
105. Ephesians 5:1
106. Romans 12:9-12
107. Ephesians 5:22-29
108. 1 Corinthians 13:8-13
109. Galatians 5:16-17
110. Joshua 22:5
111. Matthew 22:37-40
112. Jeremiah 7:23-25
113. Romans 6:4
114. Colossians 3:1-10
115. Galatians 6:10
116. Proverbs 23:6
117. Philippians 4:89
118. James 1:14
119. Ephesians 5:2
120. 1 John 1:7
121. Colossians 2:6-7
122. 1 John 1:9
123. 2 Corinthians 5:7
124. John 10:3-5
125. Psalms 37:4
126. Isaiah 30:21
127. John 14:25-26
128. Romans 8:26-27
129. 2 Corinthians 5:20
130. Proverbs 11:14
131. Hebrews 9:16
132. Jeremiah 29:11
133. 1 John 1:9